Judaism
Outside
the
Hebrew
Canon

Judaism
Outside
the
Hebrew
Canon

An Introduction to the Documents

Leonhard Rost
Translated by David E. Green

ABINGDON
Nashville

Einleitung in die alttestamentlichen Apokryphen und Pseudepigraphen
einschliesslich der grossen Qumran-Handschriften

Copyright © 1971 by Quelle & Meyer

JUDAISM OUTSIDE THE HEBREW CANON:
An Introduction to the Documents

Translation copyright © 1976 by Abingdon

Library of Congress Cataloging in Publication Data:

Rost, Leonhard, 1896-
Judaism outside the Hebrew canon.

Translation of Einleitung in die alttestamentlichen Apokryphen und
Pseudepigraphen einschliesslich der grossen Qumran-Handschriften.
Bibliography: p.
1. Apocryphal books (Old Testament)—Criticism, interpretation, etc.
2. Dead Sea scrolls.
I. Title.
BS1700.R6213   229   76-15006

ISBN 0-687-20654-5
ISBN 0-687-20653-7 pbk.

MANUFACTURED BY THE PARTHENON PRESS AT
NASHVILLE, TENNESSEE, UNITED STATES OF AMERICA

In memory of
Werner Schmeil

Contents

JUDAISM OUTSIDE THE HEBREW CANON

Foreword

When I suggested to Werner Schmeil that the tenth edition
of Sellin's *Introduction to the Old Testament* be entrusted to
my colleague Georg Fohrer, it turned out that this new
revision would cover only the Hebrew Canon of the Old
Testament. The Apocrypha and Pseudepigrapha, hereto-
fore discussed in an appendix, were to be treated in a
separate volume, which Schmeil hoped I would work on.
Preparation of the material took longer than those
concerned had expected. Except for the comprehensive
introduction by Otto Eissfeldt, which devotes 133 pages to
the Apocrypha and Pseudepigrapha together with the
related Qumran literature, no recent summary had
appeared in German giving an introduction to this
material.

It is therefore natural that I have drawn with gratitude
on Eissfeldt's work. This holds true particularly for the
bibliographies. For the most part I have not included the
monographs listed by Eissfeldt, assuming instead their
accessibility. Originally I intended to provide equally
comprehensive bibliographies, thus supplementing the
citations in Eissfeldt and bring them up to date. However,
the overwhelming flood of publications devoted not only to
the Qumran documents but also to Sirach, Tobit, and
Judith (which had to be kept within reasonable bounds),
has made it impossible to achieve this goal. Here and there
I have had to be selective, eliminating much material not
immediately relevant to problems of the type dealt with in
an introduction. For additional citations the reader should
consult bibliographical aids such as the *Elenchus biblio-
graphicus biblicus* and *Kiryat sefer*.

JUDAISM OUTSIDE THE HEBREW CANON

I have deliberately included numerous foreign publications in order to show that scholarly research is an international undertaking. Scholarship today is no longer the special privilege of certain favored nations; it depends on the cooperation of all. It is therefore both necessary and fitting to refer to this cooperative endeavor (which transcends national boundaries) even in a book like this intended for the use of students.

As a rule, the bibliographies are arranged by date of publication. Only the introduction to the discoveries at Qumran includes a survey arranged by subject, and this is intended to document a portion of the various problems that these discoveries have brought to our attention. In the introductory sections (such as the brief historical survey or the summary discussion of the intellectual milieu) the bibliographies have been limited to a few citations; the advanced scholar will not be alone in noting many omissions. This is because these sections are not meant to stand on their own, but to acquaint the reader with historical works that give access to more comprehensive studies, thus encouraging further research.

I greatly regret that I have not been able to insert references to works that appeared after I finished my manuscript—for example—J. Alberto Soggin's discussion of the additional material in the Greek Canon, in his *Introduzione all' Antico Testamento. II. Dall'esilio alla chiusura del Canone alessandrino* (1969), pp. 141–98 or Pierre Bogaert's *Apocalypse de Baruch* (1969), a study that goes far beyond the Syriac Apocalypse of Baruch.

Leonhard Rost

Erlangen, January, 1970

Introductions

W. O. E. Oesterley, *An Introduction to the Books of the Apocrypha*, 1935; C. C. Torrey, *The Apocryphal Literature*, 1945; R. H. Pfeiffer, *History of New Testament Times with an Introduction to the Apocrypha*, 1949 (especially pp. 231–522); A. Lods, *Histoire de la littérature hébraïque et juive depuis les origines jusqu'à la ruine de l'état juif*, 1950; A. Bentzen, *Introduction to the Old Testament*, 2nd ed., 1952 (especially vol. I, pp. 20–41; vol. II, pp. 218–50); B. M. Metzger, *An Introduction to the Apocrypha*, 1957; A. Belli, *Storia della litteratura ebraica, biblica e postbiblica*, Storia delle letterature di tutto il mondo 7, 1961; L. H. Brockington, *A Critical Introduction to the Apocrypha*, 1961; D. S. Russell, *Between the Testaments*, 1959; A. Robert and A. Feuillet, *Introduction à la Bible*, vol. I, 1957 (English: *Introduction to the Old Testament*, 1968); A. Weiser, *Einleitung in das Alte Testament*, 5th ed., 1963 (English: *The Old Testament, its Formation and Development*, 1961); J. M. Grintz, הספרות העברית כבתקופת פרס, *Sefer H. Albeck*, 1963; O. Eissfeldt, *Einleitung in das Alte Testament unter Einschluss der Apokryphen und Pseudepigraphen sowie der apokryphen- und pseudepigraphenartigen Qumrān-Schriften*, 3rd ed., 1964 (English: *The Old Testament, an Introduction*, 1965); H. T. Andrews, *An Introduction to the Apocryphal Books of the Old and New Testament*, 5th ed., 1964 (edited by C. H. Pfeiffer); C. Dimier, *Ce que l'Ancien Testament ne dit pas*, 1963 (English: *The Old Testament Apocrypha*, 1964); J. M. Schmidt, *Die jüdische Apokalyptik; die Geschichte ihrer Erforschung von den Anfängen bis zu den Textfunden von Qumran*, 1969; P. Prigent, *La fin de Jérusalem*, 1969; J. Barr, "Den teologiska värderingen av den efterbibliska judendomen," *SvExÅrsb*, XXXII (1967):69–78.

Abbreviations

AcOr	Acta Orientalia (Leyden)
AfO	Archiv für Orientforschung
AGA	Abhandlungen der Akademie der Wissenschaften in Göttingen
AnBibl	Analecta Biblica
Anton	Antonianum
ArLitg	Archiv für Liturgiewissenschaft
ARW	Archiv für Religionswissenschaft
AtSettBibl	Atti della Settimana Biblica
BA	Biblical Archaeologist
BAL	Berichte über die Verhandlungen der Sächsischen Akademie der Wissenschaften zu Leipzig
Bardtke I	Hans Bardtke, *Die Handschriftenfunde am Toten Meer, mit einer kurzen Einführung in die Text- und Kanonsgeschichte des Alten Testaments,* 1952
Bardtke II	*idem, Die Handschriftenfunde am Toten Meer; die Sekte von Qumran,* 1958
BASOR	Bulletin of the American Schools of Oriental Research
BETL	Bibliotheca Ephemeridarum Theologicarum Lovanensium
BHH	*Biblisch-Historisches Handwörterbuch,* Bo Reicke and Leonhard Rost, 3 vols., 1962–66
Bibl	Biblica
Biblia Sacra	*Biblia Sacra iuxta latinam vulgatam versionem ad codicum fidem,* cura et studio

13

	monachorum Abbatiae Pont. S. Hieronymi in urbe O.S.B. edita, 1951–
BibOr	Bibbia e Oriente
BiKi	Bibel und Kirche
BiLeb	Bibel und Leben
BiRes	Biblical Research
BJRL	Bulletin of the John Rylands Library
BiTod	Bible Today
BiViChr	Bible et Vie Chrétienne
BOuT	De Boeken van het Oude Testament
Brooke-McClean	A. E. Brooke, N. McClean, and H. St. J. Thackeray, *The Old Testament in Greek*, 1906–40
BSanct	Bibliotheca Sanctorum, 1962
Burrows I	M. Burrows, *The Dead Sea Scrolls*, 1955
Burrows II	M. Burrows, *More Light on the Dead Sea Scrolls*, 1958
BZ	Biblische Zeitschrift
BZAW	Beihefte zur Zeitschrift für die alttestamentliche Wissenschaft
CahRHPhR	Cahiers de la Revue d'Histoire et de Philosophie Religieuses
CBQ	Catholic Biblical Quarterly
CD	Damascus Document
CdE	Chronique d'Égypte
Charles	R. H. Charles, *The Apocrypha and Pseudepigrapha of the Old Testament in English*, 2 vols., 1913, reprinted 1968
ChQR	Church Quarterly Review
Clamer-B	L. Pirot and A. Clamer, 1946–55
CSS	Cursus Scripturae Sacrae
CuBib	Cultura Bíbbica
DJD	*Discoveries in the Judaean Desert*, 5 vols.: I: D. Barthélemy and J. T. Milik, *Qumran Cave I*, 1955

II: P. Benoit, J. T. Milik, and R. de Vaux, *Les grottes de Murabba'at,* 1961
III: M. Baillet, J. T. Milik, and R. de Vaux, *Les 'Petites Grottes' de Qumran,* 1962
IV: J. A. Sanders, *The Psalms Scroll of Qumrân Cave 11,* 1965
V: J. M. Allegro, *Qumrân Cave 4,* 1968

DA	Dissertation Abstracts
DTC	*Dictionnaire de Théologie Catholique*
Dupont-Sommer	A. Dupont-Sommer, *Les écrits Esséniens dècouvertes près de la Mer Morte,* 1959 (English: *The Essene Writings From Qumran,* 1961)
Echter-B	*Die Heilige Schrift in deutscher Übersetzung,* 1955-60
EH	Exegetisches Handbuch zum Alten Testament
Eissfeldt	O. Eissfeldt, *Einleitung in das Alte Testament unter Einschluss der Apokryphen und Pseudepigraphen sowie der apokryphen- und pseudepigraphenartigen Qumran-Schriften,* 3rd ed., 1964 (English: *The Old Testament: An Introduction,* 1965)
EncBib	*Enciclopedia Biblia*
ETL	Ephemerides Theologicae Lovanienses
EvTh	Evangelische Theologie
ExpTim	Expository Times
FAZ	Frankfurter Allgemeine Zeitung
FrancLA	Studii Biblici Franciscani Liber Annuus
Fritzsche-Grimm	O. F. Fritzsche and W. Grimm, *Kurzgefasstes exegetisches Handbuch zu den Apokryphen des AT,* 1851–60

15

JUDAISM OUTSIDE THE HEBREW CANON

FRLANT	Forschungen zur Religion und Literatur des Alten und Neuen Testaments
Fs W. Baumgartner	*Hebräische Wortforschung*, 1967
Fs W. Eichrodt	*Wort—Gebet—Glaube*, 1970
Fs S. H. Hooke	*Promise and Fulfilment*, 1963
Fs O. Michel	*Abraham unser Vater*, 1963
Fs A. H. Silver	*In the Time of Harvest*, 1963
Fs H. Thielicke	*Leben angesichts des Todes*, 1968
GerefTTs	Gereformeerd Theologisch Tijdschrift
Habermann	A. M. Habermann, *Megilloth Midbar Yehuda; The Scrolls from the Judean Desert*, 1959
Hartum	E. S. Hartum, הספרים החיצונים, 1958
HAT	Handbuch zum Alten Testament
HS	*Die Heilige Schrift des Alten Testaments*, ed. F. Feldmann and H. Herkenne
HThR	Harvard Theological Review
HUCA	Hebrew Union College Annual
IDB	*Interpreter's Dictionary of the Bible*, 1962
JAAR	Journal of the American Academy of Religion
JAOS	Journal of the American Oriental Society
JbAC	Jahrbuch für Antike und Christentum
JBL	Journal of Biblical Literature
Jerusalem-B	*La Sainte Bible traduite en français*, sous la direction de l'École Biblique de Jérusalem
JewApocrLit	S. Zeitlin et al., *Jewish Apocryphal Literature*, 1950–
JJSt	Journal of Jewish Studies
JNESt	Journal of Near Eastern Studies
JQR	Jewish Quarterly Review

JSSt	Journal of Semitic Studies
JThSt	Journal of Theological Studies
Kahana	A. Kahana, הספרים החיצונים, 2nd ed., 1956
Kautzsch	E. Kautzsch, *Die Apokryphen und Pseudepigraphen des Alten Testaments,* 1900 (1921)
KlT	Kleine Texte für theologische und philosophische Vorlesungen
KratSInAz	Kratkie Soobshchenia Instituta Narodov
LeipzSymp	H. Bardtke, ed., *Qumran-Probleme* (Vorträge des Leipziger Symposion über Qumran-Probleme, 1961), 1963
LifeSpir	*Life of the Spirit*
LondQHolbR	London Quarterly and Holborn Review
LXX	Septuagint
Maier	J. Maier, *Die Texte vom Toten Meer,* 2 vols., 1960
Mél E. Tisserant	*Mélanges Eugene Tisserant,* Studi e Testi, 231–37, 1964
MGWJ	Monatsschrift für Geschichte und Wissenschaft des Judentums
MIOF	Mitteilungen des Instituts für Orientforschung
ModChm	Modern Churchman
Montserrat-B	*La Biblia: Versió dels Textos Originals i Comentari pels Monjos de Montserrat*
NAWG	Nachrichten der Akademie der Wissenschaften zu Göttingen
NedTTs	Nederlands Theologisch Tijdschrift
NewCathEnc	*New Catholic Encyclopedia*
NF	Neue Folge

17

JUDAISM OUTSIDE THE HEBREW CANON

NGG	Nachrichten von der Gesellschaft der Wissenschaften zu Göttingen
NS	New Series
NT	Novum Testamentum
OTS	Oudtestamentische Studien
PalCl	Palestra del Clero
Rahlfs	A. Rahlfs, *Septuaginta*
RB	Revue Biblique (Vols. 50–52 = Vivre et Penser, 1–3)
RBibIt	Rivista Biblica Italiana
RBiCalz	Revista Biblica (R. Calzada)
RClAfr	Revue du Clergé Africain
RÉLat	Revue des Études Latines
RÉSlav	Revue des Études Slaves
RGG	*Die Religion in Geschichte und Gegenwart,* 3rd ed., 1957–65
RHMédHébr	Revue d'Histoire de la Médecine Hébraïque
RHR	Revue de l'Histoire des Religions
Riessler	P. Riessler, *Altjüdisches Schrifttum ausserhalb der Bibel,* 1928, reprinted 1966
RoczTKan	*Roczniki teologiczno-Kanoniczne*
RR	Review of Religion
RSR	Recherches de Science Religieuse
RStO	Rivista degli Studi Orientali
RuBi	Ruch Biblijny i Liturgiczny
SaBi	La Sacra Bibbia (Turin)
SAM	Sitzungsberichte der Bayerischen Akademie der Wissenschaften
Sem	Semitica
ST	Studia theologica
Studii Teol	Studii Teologice
StUNT	Studien zur Umwelt des Neuen Testaments

SVT	Supplements to Vetus Testamentum
SvExÅrsb	Svensk Exegetisk Årsbok
Swete	H. B. Swete, *The Old Testament in Greek According to the Septuagint,* 3 vols.
TGegw	Theologie der Gegenwart in Auswahl
ThQ	Theologische Quartalschrift
ThR	Theologische Rundschau
ThreskEthEnk	Θρησκευτικὴ καὶ ἠθικὴ ἐγκυκλοπαιδεία
TLon	Theology (London)
TriererThSt	Trierer Theologische Studien
TriererThZ	Trierer Theologische Zeitschrift
ThZBas	Theologische Zeitschrift (Basel)
VD	Verbum Domini
VizVrem	Vizantij Vremennik
VT	Vetus Testamentum
Vulgata	R. Weber, *Biblia Sacra iuxta Vulgatam Versionem,* 1969
WBTh	Wiener Beiträge zur Theologie
WC	Westminster Commentaries
WZJena	Wissenschaftliche Zeitschrift (Jena)
WZKM	Wiener Zeitschrift für die Kunde des Morgenlandes
Yad.	Yadayim (Mishnah)
ZÄS	Zeitschrift für Ägyptische Sprache und Altertumskunde
ZAW	Zeitschrift für die alttestamentliche Wissenschaft
ZDPV	Zeitschrift des Deutschen Palästina-Vereins
ZKG	Zeitschrift für Kirchengeschichte
ZNW	Zeitschrift für die neutestamentliche Wissenschaft
ZThK	Zeitschrift für Theologie und Kirche

I. INTRODUCTION

The Hebrew Canon

Besides the Introductions already mentioned, see also E. Sellin and G. Fohrer, *Einleitung in das Alte Testament*, 11th ed., 1969 (English: *Introduction to the Old Testament*, 1968); O. Kaiser, *Einleitung in das Alte Testament*, 1969.

G. C. Aalders, *Oud-testamentische Kanoniek*, 1952; R. Martin-Achard, *Approche de l'Ancien Testament*, 1962 (English: *An Approach to the Old Testament*, 1965); F. F. Bruce, *The Books and the Parchments*, 2nd ed., 1963; K. Koch, *Das Buch der Bücher*, Verständliche Wissenschaft, 83, 1963 (English: *The Book of Books*, 1968); G. M. Perella, *Introduzione generale alla Sacra Bibbia*, 3rd ed., 1963; B. J. Bamberger, *The Bible, a Modern Jewish Approach*, 2nd ed., 1963; H. Höpfl, *Introductio specialis in Vetus Testamentum*, ed. 6. quam curavit S. Bovo (= vol. 2 of his *Introductio in sacros utriusque testamenti libros*), 1963; H. H. Rowley, *The Growth of the Old Testament*, 1963; N. Appel, *Kanon und Kirche*, 1964; G. L. Archer, Jr., *A Survey of Old Testament Introduction*, 1964; K. Dronkert, *Gids voor het OT*, Vol. I, 1965; R. Mayer, *Einleitung in das Alte Testament*, I. Teil: Allgemeine Einleitung, 1965; G. G. Yates, *A Guide to the Old Testament*, 1965; C. Kuhl, *Inleiding to het OT*, 1965; I. H. Eybers, "Historical Evidence on the Canon of the Old Testament with Special Reference to the Qumran Sect," dissertation, Duke, 1966 (abstract in *DA*, XXVII [1966/67]: 1910–A); A. C. Sundberg, Jr., "The Old Testament: A Christian Canon," *CBQ*, XXX (1968):143–55; J. C. H. Lebram, "Aspekte der alttestamentlichen Kanonbildung," *VT*, XVIII (1968):173–89.

JUDAISM OUTSIDE THE HEBREW CANON

The terms "apocrypha," "pseudepigrapha," and "extracanonical writings" were used in various senses during the course of two thousand years of Christian history before they acquired the meaning they have today. But in the period when most of the writings now represented by these categories came into being, there was as yet no official canon, or, as Mishnah Yadayim iv. 6 puts it, there was no fixed group of כתבי קדש, holy scriptures. Even in the time around A.D. 100, when the Mishnah achieved its final form, the scholars were arguing whether or not to include the Song of Songs and Ecclesiastes (Qoheleth) among the Holy Scriptures. The argument was finally resolved by a decision in favor of their inclusion (Mishnah Yad. iii. 5cd). The Dead Sea manuscripts, especially those from the caves at Qumran, dating from the period 150 B.C.–A.D. 70, show that at that time there was no sharp distinction between holy scriptures and those reckoned less holy. Otherwise it would have been impossible to employ the same esteemed form of script used to copy Isaiah or Genesis to copy Sirach, Enoch, the Book of Jubilees, the Testament of Levi, and the Testament of Naphtali; likewise, strict observance of the distinction recognizable in the Mishnah between writings that make the hands unclean, and are therefore sacred, and secular writings that do not make the hands unclean (Mishnah Yad. iii. 5) would have made it impossible for the fragment 11Q to include with the Psalms certain hymns later excluded as apocryphal or pseudepigraphal.

To be sure, as early a document as the prologue of Sirach (about 190 B.C.) distinguishes "the Law and the Prophets and the others that followed them" or "the Law and the Prophets and the other books of our fathers" as three groups of traditional writings "on account of which we should praise Israel for instruction and wisdom." But Sirach's grandfather was led to set his own wisdom on a par with these in a work that later was not included in the Hebrew Canon (the *hebraica veritas* of Luther), and until very recently, was known only through the Greek translation in the Septuagint. An extensive portion of Sirach in Hebrew, written in stichs (which indicates that the scribe took great pains with his work), was among the few manuscript fragments found at Masada; this discovery attests to the high esteem in which this work was held by the Zealots in the first century c.e.

On the other hand, Philo of Alexandria records in section 25 of his *Vita contemplativa* (middle of the first century c.e.) that the therapeutae in their seclusion limited their reading to "laws and words revealed through prophets and psalms and the other things that serve to increase knowledge and devotion and lead to perfection," thus revealing that the therapeutae were familiar with a tripartite collection of scriptures that corresponded to the later three divisions of the Hebrew Canon. It is impossible to say anything definite about what particular writings belonged to the third section or about its scope, however. Josephus makes a clearer statement in this regard in i. 8 of his *Contra Apionem* (*ca.* A.D. 95). Following a long discussion in which he seeks to demonstrate, in part by example, how untrustworthy and contradictory are the accounts of the Egyptians, Babylonians, and Greeks, he states: "We do not have tens of thousands of mutually contradictory and polemical books, but just twenty-two, which contain the records of the entire period and are rightly accounted trustworthy." Unfortunately he does not list the individual books, so that there are two possibilities: one must either count Ruth with Judges and Lamentations with Jeremiah to arrive at the number given, or one must assume that Josephus' collection did not include the Song of Songs and Ecclesiastes, which were still disputed. The author of IV Ezra, writing about the same time, states that Ezra released twenty-four books for publication while keeping secret seventy additional writings that had been revealed to him; there can be no question that he is referring to the twenty-four books of the Tanach, consisting of Torah, Nevi'im, and Ketuvim.

It is dubious whether both Josephus and the author of

IV Ezra were already acquainted with the arrangement of books found in the Hebrew Bible, for the Babylonian Talmud (Baba bathra 14*b*), dating from the fifth century, still lists the books in a different order. The present arrangement of the Hebrew Bible came into being when the five festal Megilloth (Heb. *megillah*, "scroll") were grouped together: Song of Songs (Passover); Ruth (Feast of Weeks); Lamentations (Ninth of Ab); Ecclesiastes (Feast of Booths); and Esther (Purim). In other words, it derives from the need for a systematic arrangement.

In summary, while we can say that the acceptance of Deuteronomy as authoritative under Josiah in 621 B.C. marked the first step on the road to canonization, it is also true that the Jewish community did not feel the need for a clear definition as to which traditional writings of the fathers were sacred until the first century C.E. The need to erect defenses against the burgeoning literature of the various sects, as well as against that of nascent Christianity, played a role that can no longer be estimated with accuracy. In the Qumran community there was a real danger that the *sēfer hāhāgû* (CD x. 6; xiii. 2) or *sēfer hāhāgî* (1QSa i. 2; cf. 1QH xi. 2, 21)—perhaps to be identified with the Thanksgiving Scroll—would be included amongst the normative scriptures.

A norm for the selection of those writings that should belong to the Canon is given by Josephus in *Contra Apionem* i. 8. Having designated the Pentateuch as the work of Moses, Josephus continues: "From the death of Moses until Artaxerxes, the successor to Xerxes, king of the Persians, the prophets who followed after Moses recorded their deeds in thirteen books. The remaining four [books] comprise hymns to God and rules of ethical conduct for men." In the words of the Babylonian Talmud (Baba bathra 14*b*, 15*a*), we read: "Moses wrote his book together with the Balaam passage (Num. 22–24) and Job; Joshua wrote his book and the eight verses of the Torah (Deut. 34:5-12); Samuel wrote his book and the book of Judges and Ruth; David wrote the book of Psalms through ten elders, through Adam the first, through Melchizedek, and through Abraham and through Moses and through Heman and through Jeduthun and through Asaph and through the three Korahites; Jeremiah wrote his book and the book of Kings and Lamentations; Hezekiah and his company wrote (the catchword is *yamšaq*)[1] the book of Isaiah, Proverbs, the Song of Songs, and Ecclesiastes; the men of the Great Assembly wrote (catchword *qandag*)[2] Ezekiel, the Twelve Prophets, Daniel, and the Esther Scroll; Ezra wrote his book and the genealogies of Chronicles." This means that the authors of the books are assigned to the period from Moses to Ezra, which is the same period referred to by Josephus as "from Moses to Artaxerxes I." IV Ezra has the lost books dictated to Ezra; thus he takes the final figure from the period of Artaxerxes I and attributes all the books to him. Unhistorical as these claims may be, they clearly reveal the purpose behind them: no book written after Ezra the priest, the scribe of the law of the God of heaven (Ezra 7:12), can be considered Holy Scripture. Tosefta Sota 13. 2 goes on to give the reason: the Holy Spirit departed after the death of Haggai, Zechariah, and Malachi. Thus Judaism defined the limits of the canon that was and still is accepted within the Jewish community.

The documents contained in this canon cannot in reality be dated totally within the framework of the period from Moses to Artaxerxes I or Ezra, as any Introduction to the Old Testament will show.

The Greek Canon and the "Apocrypha"

Besides the Introductions and the works cited in section I above, see also: P. Sacchi, "Il testo dei Settanta nella Problematica più recente," *Atene e Roma*, NS IX (1964): 148–58; H. H. Rowley, *The Origin and Significance of the Apocrypha*, Christian Knowledge Booklets, 1967; C. Stuhlmueller, "Apocrypha of the OT," in *NewCathEnc*

[1] *yamšaq* = *yᵉšāyāhû, mᵉšālîm, šîr haššîrîm, qōhelet*.
[2] *qandag* = *yᵉḥezqēl, šᵉnêm 'āsār, dānî'ēl, megillat estēr*.

25

JUDAISM OUTSIDE THE HEBREW CANON

(1967), II: 396–404; S. Jellicoe, *The Septuagint and Modern Study*, 1968; H. B. Swete, *An Introduction to the Old Testament in Greek*, rev. by R. R. Ottley with an appendix containing the Letter of Aristeas ed. by H. St. J. Thackeray, 1968.

During the Exile and the Diaspora, and then upon the return of the Jews to their homeland in Judah, the fact of the Persian Empire made it natural for the Jews to use Official Aramaic as a *lingua franca*. This is attested by the Aramaic sections of the book of Ezra and the book of Daniel, and, for the Egyptian Diaspora, by the Elephantine papyri. In similar fashion, incorporation into the empire of Alexander the Great and into the Hellenistic states of the Diadochi into which it disintegrated meant coming to terms with the Hellenism of the victor. Especially in Egypt, this led to the development of a Jewish literature in Greek. Philo of Alexandria (about 15 B.C. to A.D. 45) deserves special mention in this context.

Probably as early as the third century B.C. a need was felt to make the Torah accessible in Greek translation to a Jewish stratum no longer sufficiently competent in Hebrew. Presumably the lections were translated into Greek verse by verse when the people assembled for worship, a procedure analogous to that described in Nehemiah 8:8, where Levites translated into Aramaic as Ezra read the Torah. These ad hoc extemporaneous translations led to fixed written versions, which were finally replaced by an authorized translation, at first comprising only the Torah. It, too, was the focal point of synagogue worship, but the translation was probably undertaken for constitutional reasons—in the Hellenistic state of the Ptolemies the purpose of the translation was to perform the function performed by Ezra's Torah in the Persian Empire, namely to document the privileges that had to be guaranteed for the practice of a form of worship different from the Hellenistic state religion. This is probably the real background of the elaborate account in the Letter of Aristeas. According to Mishnah Yadayim iv. 5, scrolls in square script written in ink on leather were the only ones that could be used for liturgical purposes. The vehement insistance on this restriction shows the popularity of manuscripts—and probably of the translations into Aramaic and Greek as well—that did not fulfill the requirements of the Pharisees around A.D. 100. It also shows that manuscripts in the archaic Hebrew script, written before rabbinic approval, were not considered trustworthy. This applies, for example, to the archaic Leviticus manuscript from Qumran; but the other biblical manuscripts from the Qumran caves also show that the process of defining a text with universal acceptance, associated with the formation of the Canon, was only gradually accomplished.

As the preface to Sirach shows, besides the works that were later included in the Hebrew Canon, other books were translated that were highly esteemed in certain smaller or larger circles and were read for religious edification until the end of the first century C.E. Some of them gained acceptance into the collections of sacred books that, according to the evidence of the great Greek uncials of the fourth century, were borrowed by the Christian church on Egyptian soil. They would certainly not have been adopted had they not been part of a Jewish collection. Only such an explanation as this can account for the inclusion of these books on an equal footing with the Hebrew Canon, which, in its original language, became inaccessible to the Christians with the passage of time. In Codex Vaticanus (B), I Ezra follows Chronicles; in Codex Alexandrinus (A), it follows Judith. In B and A, Judith and Tobit follow Esther; to them are appended additions to the latter book. Baruch and the Letter of Jeremiah follow Jeremiah; the Song of the Three Young Men, Susanna, and Bel and the Dragon follow the book of Daniel. Only in A are the two books of Maccabees found following Ezra; they are not contained in B. But Sirach and the Wisdom of Solomon are found in both uncials, and the Prayer of Manasseh appears among the odes appended to the Psalter. Only II Maccabees and the Wisdom of Solomon were originally written in Greek; all the other writings outside the Hebrew corpus had Hebrew originals, part or all of which have been preserved in various cases.

Here we can only single out the most important transitions in the subsequent history of this Greek corpus of sacred books. It is impossible to say when this Greek translation fell into disuse among the Jews since there exists no evidence on this point. About A.D. 100 in any case, the Mishnah adjudged holy only the Hebrew text written in the prescribed form; it alone could be used in the cult. When and how this regulation came into force is beyond our ken. The Greek Christian communities continued to make use of the more inclusive Greek corpus of sacred books. This Greek corpus is attested in the earliest uncials—B[1] and A[2].

Sinaiticus has not been preserved in its entirety. Since, however, it includes I and II Maccabees, it very probably was in general agreement with B and A with respect to the books included. Nevertheless, those books not found in the Hebrew corpus were termed "deuterocanonical." The synods of Hippo (393) and Carthage (397 and 419), together with Augustine, Innocent I, and Gelasius, show that the Western Church did not make this distinction, although Jerome (340/350–420) distinguished the *libri canonici* of the Hebrew corpus from the *libri apocryphi*, the "apocryphal books." In later times, also, objections were

---

[1] The earliest collection of sacred scriptures in Greek is the library of eleven papyrus codices known as the Chester Beatty Collection. They probably represent the stock of biblical scriptures possessed by a fourth-century Christian community, or at least the major and most valuable portion. They were discovered in 1931 in a cemetery or in the ruins of a church in the vicinity of Aphroditopolis (Tepyeh, about twenty-five miles south of Memphis on the east bank of the Nile). Besides Genesis, Numbers, Deuteronomy, Isaiah, Jeremiah, Ezekiel, Daniel, and Esther, the collection also includes Sirach and portions of Enoch. It is therefore only partially preserved. The inclusion of Enoch shows that its canonicity had not yet been settled. That some considered it canonical is shown by a citation in verse 14 of the Letter of Jude.

[2] Codex A concluded with the Psalms of Solomon, which were never considered canonical but do belong to the Pseudepigrapha.

raised to individual books of the Apocrypha, especially by the Western Church. Finally the Council of Trent decreed in 1546 that all the apocryphal books—i.e., Tobias, Judith (after Nehemiah = II Esdras), Liber Sapientiae, Ecclesiasticus (after Canticum canticorum), Baruch (after Jeremias), Macchabaeorum primus et secundus (after Malachias)—were to be considered canonical, while Oratio Manasse and Esdrae liber terius et quartus, standing outside the Canon, were appended to the New Testament.

In the Eastern Church, the Council in Trullo (692) had already adopted the decision of Carthage (397 and 419), thus recognizing the apocryphal books as canonical. Finally the Council of Jerusalem in 1672 declared only Tobit, Judith, Sirach, and the Wisdom of Solomon to be canonical.

Thus the apocryphal books do not present any problem in either the Greek or the Latin Canon. The problem became acute, however, in the churches of the Reformation, since Luther, influenced by the humanist motto *ad fontes* ("to the sources") and relying on *hebraica veritas,* defined the Hebrew corpus as canonical and relegated Jerome's *libri ecclesiastici* to an appendix with the title "Apocrypha, that is, books not to be held equal to Holy Scripture, but still useful and profitable to read." Under this rubric he included the following, preferring the text of the Vulgate: Judith, die Weisheit Salomonis, das Buch Tobie, das Buch Jesus Syrach, der Prophet Baruch, das erste Buch Maccabeorum, das ander Buch der Maccabeer, Stücke in Esther, Historia von der Susanne und Daniel, von dem Bel zu Babel, vom Drachen zu Babel, das Gebet Asarie: Dani III, der Gesang der dreien Menner im Fewr, Dani III, das Gebet Manasses, des Königes Juda (H. E. Bindseil und H. A. Niemeyer, *Dr. Martin Luther's Bibelüber-setzung,* 5. Theil, 1853). He thus rejected III Esdras, III Maccabees, Baruch, and the Letter of Jeremiah, which are included in the Latin Canon. These books, however, are generally included in Introductions to the Apocrypha.

JUDAISM OUTSIDE THE HEBREW CANON

The Reformed churches recognize only the Hebrew Canon, and for this reason most Protestant editions of the Bible omit the Apocrypha.

The "Pseudepigrapha"

J. Bonsirven, *La Bible Apocryphe en marge de l'Ancien Testament,* Textes pour l'Histoire Sacré choisis et présentés par Daniel-Rops, 1953; C. Albeck, "Agadot im Lichte der Pseudepigraphen," *MGWJ,* LXXXIII (1939 [ed. 1963]): 162–69; *De gammeltestamentlige pseudepigrafer,* i oversaettelse med inledning og noter ved Hammershaimb, J. Munck, B. Noack, and P. Seidelin, 4 volumes, 1963; M. Philonenko, J. C. Picard, J. M. Rosenstiehl, and F. Schmidt, *Pseudépigraphes de l'Ancien Testament et manuscrits de la Mer Morte,* I, 1967; A. M. Denis and M. de Jonge, ed., *Introduction aux pseudépigraphes grecs d'Ancien Testament,* Studia in Veteris Testamenti Pseudepigrapha, 1, 1970.

The Apocrypha is a corpus of Jewish documents, some from Palestine and some from the Diaspora, dating from the third to the first century B.C. These works were probably not excluded from the collection of books recognized within the Jewish community until after the nascent Christian church had accepted the Greek Canon of the Old Testament. The pseudepigrapha, by contrast, are Jewish writings that were accepted only within certain groups, although they date from almost the same period as the Apocrypha. These books never achieved a status like that of the canonical books either in the imperial church of the East or in the Western Church. This literature was preserved only (like Pseudo-Philo) in a restricted portion of the medieval Western Church or (like Enoch and other books) on the fringes of Christendom, among the Abyssinians, the Copts, and the Syrian churches. Even there they never belonged to the Canon, although the Epistle of Jude in the New Testament quotes the Assumption of Moses in verse 9 and Enoch in verses 14–15, and the Greek Codex Alexandrinus concludes with the Psalms of Solomon.

The definition of the pseudepigrapha is vague. If we go by the actual meaning of the word, we are talking about writings that were circulated pseudonymously. The nominal authors were usually famous religious figures of the past, like Adam, Enoch, Moses, Elijah, Jeremiah, Baruch, or Solomon; a later author would hope to gain a hearing by publishing under such a name. But the Jewish extracanonical literature (P. Riessler) includes other works that are not covered by the term "pseudepigrapha": some are of anonymous origin, others are not placed in the mouth of any great figure of the past. Above all, the notion has been extended by newly discovered works from the same period. Of course it is possible to argue about what works should be included. Inclusion of the Aboth (Pirke Aboth) can be supported on the grounds that it is a collection of wisdom aphorisms; its exclusion can be supported on the grounds that it belongs to the Mishnah, being an integral part (the ninth tractate of the fourth seder Nezikin) of this systematic legal compendium growing out of the Torah. The inclusion of Ahikar, as suggested by R. H. Charles, must remain dubious because its autobiographical wisdom is probably foreign—more specifically, Babylonian; Ahikar's only connection with the Jewish Diaspora community in Upper Egypt is evidenced by its discovery in Aramaic translation with the Elephantine papyri.

The number of Qumran documents that should be included among the pseudepigrapha remains questionable. Apart from the biblical texts, two types of documents are involved. On the one hand, there are fragments of texts that in the past have generally been included among the Apocrypha and pseudepigrapha—for example, Sirach and Judith. On the other hand, there are documents that were so much the special property of a particular group that they could never have circulated outside of it. These include the Manual of Discipline (1QS, Sa, Sb), the War Scroll (1QM), the Hymns (1QH), and some others that are preserved only in small fragments. The most likely candidate for a place among the pseudepigrapha is the

Genesis Apocryphon (1QGenApok); it can be placed alongside the well-known Book of Jubilees, which it resembles. On the other hand, some of the pseudepigrapha (like Enoch and the Book of Jubilees just mentioned) have turned out to be so closely related to the ideology and special institutions (such as the calendar) of Qumran that their authors, though they may not have been among those dwelling in the monastery or the caves or even been buried in the cemetery at Qumran, must at least have considered Qumran to be their spiritual home. It is therefore probably necessary to follow O. Eissfeldt in including the Qumran documents in the group of those to be discussed as pseudepigrapha, although some of them—the regulations and liturgical documents of the sect itself, together with the pesher literature—can only be treated as appendices.[1]

Recent treatments of this topic illustrate the increase in the pseudepigrapha and the related literature of late Judaism. In the second volume of Kautzsch's collection of the Apocrypha and pseudepigrapha, he includes twelve pseudepigrapha: the Letter of Aristeas, the Book of Jubilees, the Martyrdom of Isaiah, the Psalms of Solomon, so-called IV Maccabees, the Sibylline Oracles, the Book of Enoch, the Assumption of Moses, IV Ezra, the Apocalypse of Baruch (subdivided into the Syriac Apocalypse and the Greek Apocalypse), the Testaments of the Twelve Patriarchs, and the Life of Adam and Eve. R. H. Charles adds Pirke Aboth from the Mishnah, Ahikar, and the Damascus Document, which had been published by Schechter three years earlier. P. Riessler drops Ahikar but adds other works and fragments not included by Charles, arriving at a total of sixty-one documents.

The same situation prevails in the Introductions. In the first edition of E. Sellin's Introduction (1910), he restricts himself to eleven documents: the Letter of Aristeas, the

---

[1] The Damascus Document, which must have been very popular at Qumran in view of the large number of copies made of it, had a separate fate. It was also discovered by S. Schechter in the genizah at Cairo, in the remnants of manuscripts dating from the tenth and eleventh centuries.

INTRODUCTION

Book of Jubilees, the Book of Enoch, the Assumption of
Moses, the Vision of Isaiah, the Apocalypse of Baruch, IV
Ezra, the Testaments of the Twelve Patriarchs, the
Sibylline Oracles, the Psalms of Solomon, and the Odes of
Solomon. The ninth edition (1959) adds several Qumran
documents: the Damascus Document, the War Scroll, the
Manual of Discipline, the Thanksgiving Scroll, and the
commentary on Habakkuk. A. Weiser does not deal with
the pseudepigrapha until his second edition (1949), when
he discusses fifteen works, among them the Damascus
Document, under this heading. In the fifth edition he adds
the Manual of Discipline, the War Scroll, and the Hymns
from Qumran, together with a survey of the Dead Sea
Scrolls. In his first edition (1934) O. Eissfeldt restricts
himself to fourteen documents; in his third edition he adds
a comprehensive survey of the Qumran discoveries in nine
paragraphs.

This Introduction will deal with the fourteen documents
termed pseudepigrapha by Kautzsch, Sellin, Weiser,
Eissfeldt, and others, together with [Pseudo-] Philo's
Historia mundi and the major Qumran documents, albeit
without attempting to compete with Eissfeldt's survey. The
Story of Ahikar is appended—following Charles.

Historical Summary

E. Schürer, *Geschichte des jüdischen Volkes im Zeitalter Jesu
Christi,* reprinted 1964 (English: *A History of the Jewish People
in the Time of Jesus,* ed. and introd. by N. N. Glatzer, 1962;
History of the Jewish People in the Age of Jesus Christ, 1973–);
M. A. Beek, *Geschiedenis van Israel van Abraham tot Bar
Kochba,* 1957 (English: *Concise History of Israel from Abraham
to the Bar Cochba Rebellion,* 1963); F. F. Bruce, *Israel and the
Nations,* 1963; E. L. Ehrlich, *Geschichte Israels von den
Anfängen bis zur Zerstörung des Tempels,* 1958 (English: *A
Concise History of Israel from the Earliest Times to the Destruction
of the Temple,* 1963); M. Noth, *Geschichte Israels,* 5th ed.,
1963 (English: *The History of Israel,* 2nd ed., 1960); A.

JUDAISM OUTSIDE THE HEBREW CANON

Tcherikover, היהודים בתקופת ההלניסטית, 1963 (English: Hellenistic Civilization and the Jews, 1959); *idem*, היודים במצרים בתקופת ההלניסטית הרומנית לאור הפאפירולוגיה, 1963; W. Foerster, *Neutestamentliche Zeitgeschichte*, 1956 (English: *From the Exile to Christ*, 1964); B. Reicke, *Neutestamentliche Zeitgeschichte*, 1965 (English: *The New Testament Era*, 1968); M. Avi-Yonah, *The Holy Land from the Persian to the Arab Conquests*, 1966; J. Morgenstern, "The HASIDIM—Who Were They?" *HUCA*, XXXVIII (1967):59–73; D. S. Russell, *The Jews from Alexander to Herod*, 1967; C. Thoma, "Auswirkungen des jüdischen Krieges gegen Rom (66–70/73 n. Chr.) auf das rabbinische Judentum," *BZ*, NF XII (1968):30–54, 186–210; B. Z. Wacholder, "Biblical Chronology in the Hellenistic World Chronicles," *HThR*, LXI (1968):451–81; H. Mantel, "The Causes of the Bar Kochba Revolt," *JQR*, LVIII (1968):224–42, 274–96.

The Apocrypha and pseudepigrapha came into being between the third century B.C. and the first century A.D. This was a period characterized by wars, rebellions, and successful or unsuccessful wars of liberation; by petty intrigues and assassinations; by firm adherence to the Law of Moses which led to spiritual anguish and corporal suffering and oppression; and by the invasion of Hellenism not only as a movement opening new intellectual horizons, but as a tendency for rulers to ignore the individual and cultivate an insatiable lust for power. The tiny group of Jews clustering around the temple at Jerusalem constituted only a fraction of Jewry, a fraction that grew smaller and smaller with the passage of time. Most of the Jews lived, by choice or by necessity, in the Diaspora. Thus they were in the midst of alien peoples who often exhibited little understanding of Jewish distinctiveness and frequently reacted with intolerance or even hatred to the Jews' alleged *odium humani generis* (Tacitus *Annales* xv. 44). This attitude resulted in oppression and persecution, which in turn evoked the chimera of messianic expectations. Here and there such hopes led those who were under the spell of such illusions into crusades against both foreign rule (perceived as oppressive) and those members of the Jewish community who could not assent to follow this gospel because they saw how senseless it was. Sectarian groups arose who preached nonviolence (because they expected God to take care of everything) and who claimed that they could see in the mounting oppression itself signs of the end. The early Christians and even Jesus were not spared such accusations, judgments, and temptations.

Under two hundred years of Persian rule, the Jews, the descendants of the Judeans deported to Babylon by Nebuchadrezzar in 597 and 586 B.C., had been able to enjoy a life that was by and large uneventful. Therefore only a portion of them had taken advantage of Cyrus's edict, issued at Ecbatana in 537, permitting reconstruction of the Temple at government expense and the associated privileges. A messianic movement growing up around Zerubbabel, a descendant of David, and Joshua, the high priest, sometime around 520 miscarried. By 516 the Temple had been completely rebuilt, albeit shabbily. Disputes between the Jews and their neighbors, especially the Samaritans, were suppressed by the Persians, often in favor of the returnees, who had friends at court in the descendants of the exiles who had stayed behind in Mesopotamia.

We know two of these by name: Ezra, "the scribe of the law of the God of heaven" (in other words, the head of the office for the religious affairs of the Jews in the Persian Empire), and Nehemiah ben Hacaliah, cupbearer of King Artaxerxes I (465–424). Whether Ezra also served under Artaxerxes I or under Artaxerxes II (402–358) is disputed, but much evidence suggests that Ezra's work followed that of Nehemiah. Nehemiah received twelve years' leave from royal service to rebuild the Jerusalem city walls, which he carried out by assigning portions of the work to the leading citizens, a system (Greek *leitourgia*, "liturgy") attested for the same period in the construction of Greek city walls. The rebuilt wall made the inhabitants of the city more secure. Nehemiah also increased the population living inside the city, compelling some to move and encouraging others to do so; he helped the lower classes by remitting debts; he enjoined observance of the sabbath, and helped establish stricter criteria in the question of mixed marriages. During this time and during a second stay in Jerusalem that followed a lengthy interim at the royal court, he was able to claim the title of satrap; he was therefore able to restrict the rights of the satrap residing in Samaria, who had until Nehemiah's arrival exercised authority over Jerusalem, and gain for the Jewish temple community a status that was politically secure. This policy of bringing independence to the Jews culminated in their commitment to obey the Torah of Yahweh—that is, the Law of Moses—under Ezra. Thus all the Jews in the Persian Empire, whether in Jerusalem or the Diaspora, were able, with Persian approbation, to live by both the civil and religious law of their forefathers, a situation whose effects have lasted to the present (cf. *Verbannung und Heimkehr* [1961], pp. 301–7). This brought to an end a kind of consolidation of the Jews within the Persian Empire; until Alexander the Great invaded Asia and Africa, they were able, minor grievances aside, to enjoy a certain security.

The transition to the world empire of Alexander the Great meant not only a change of sovereignty, but also incorporation into the realm of the Hellenism unleashed by the campaign of Alexander—that is, the increasing penetration of the Greek intellectual world into the East. How enormous was the difference between the cautious administration of the Persians and the missionary zeal of the Hellenistic enlightenment was first seen under the rule of the Diadochi (the successors of Alexander) and the states they governed. The people did not become aware of the new situation during the amazing campaign of the victorious Macedonian, but only after his early death at Babylon in 323. The wars of the Diadochi that immediately broke out divided the empire into successor states under

Macedonian leadership. Those of primary interest to us are Syria, under the Seleucids, and Egypt, under the Ptolemies; they were the two that alternately claimed hegemony over Palestine until the Romans appeared in the Near East. In Jerusalem, however, were located the religious foci of the Jews—the Temple and (the highest spiritual dignitary) the high priest, who was responsible not only for the cult, but also for civil law to the extent that the Torah had served this latter purpose since Ezra. He was the guardian of the ancestral Law and thus the leader of the Jews—including those living in the Diaspora.

In the struggle for Palestine, the Egyptian Ptolemies first gained the upper hand. They considered Palestine a springboard for further penetration into Asia Minor and a bastion for defense of their copper mines on the Sinai peninsula. Ptolemy I Lagi (305–283/82) took Jewish captives to Egypt from Jerusalem and Judea and then forced Jews to settle in Egyptian garrison cities, apparently without any concern for Jewish internal affairs. Not until he was succeeded by Ptolemy II Philadelphus (283–246) did the Jews manage to regain the privileges they had had under the Persians in the altered situation of a Hellenistic empire. The *ethnos* of the Jews received permission to live by their ancestral laws. Very probably it was to obtain this privilege that the Torah was translated into Greek and thus introduced to the Western world. This might well constitute the nucleus of the highly elaborate narrative in the Letter of Aristeas. While the Ptolemies ruled, there was no change in this privileged status however much Egyptian military conflict with the Seleucids affected the security of the people living in Palestine. The high priest also represented the *gens Judaea* in the political realm, despite the hegemony of the Ptolemies.

But another danger to the Jews was slowly and insidiously coming into being—schism. Hellenism was culturally superior to Judaism and built upon totally different principles; incorporation of the Jews into such a world naturally meant assimilation and dislocation in many areas.

37

It is understandable that the ruling circles were more responsive to these stimuli than the poorer classes. The differences were not yet extreme. In the course of the conflicts between Egypt and Syria, however, Antiochus III (223–187) forced the Egyptians under Scopas, who commanded the army on behalf of Ptolemy V (203–181/80) (who was still in his minority) to relinquish Palestine. This took place in 198 B.C. at the Battle of Panion. The situation of the Jews living in the vicinity of the Jerusalem Temple thereupon deteriorated, since a territorial boundary now separated them from the strong Egyptian Diaspora. At the same time, the rift between the Jews and the Samaritans deepened and deepened, as well, between the *Hasidim* ("devout ones"), who maintained the traditional law and extended it by means of interpretation, and the Hellenists, who were open to innovation and ready for more or less extensive assimilation. The Syrian garrisons and the Hellenistic city-states of Palestine that enjoyed the favor of the Syrians made the situation even more difficult, for there could be no question of a reasonably unified territory for the Jews to live in. When Antiochus IV Epiphanes (175–163) came to the throne the situation came to a head. The Hellenists in Jerusalem felt strong enough to ask their ruler to have their city governed by Hellenistic law. He gladly acceded. But the high priest Onias was replaced by his brother Menelaus, who favored the Hellenists; a Syrian garrison was stationed in the citadel overlooking the Temple area from the north; and finally in December of 168 the cult of Zeus was introduced in the Jerusalem Temple. Worship of this god was also made compulsory in the rural villages. These events provoked a movement among those classes of people who still clung to Yahwism; all that was necessary for them to leap into action was a sign. This was provided by Mattathias, a priest from Modein: he killed the agent of Archelaus and destroyed the altar of Zeus in his home town. Now the resistance had its leader. Mattathias died in 166/165, but his sons Judas (166/165–160), Simon (160/159–142/141), and Jonathan (142/141–135/134) continued what he had begun. The struggle against Syrian rule and the Jewish Hellenists was bitter. But in December of 164 it was possible to reconsecrate the altar of the Jerusalem Temple. The interlude of the Zeus cult had come to an end. But the Syrian garrison stayed in the citadel until May of 142. Antiochus Epiphanes had died in 164 of an illness he contracted after an unsuccessful campaign at the eastern boundary of his empire. But the Syrians continued to pose a threat, especially because pretenders constantly disputed the succession to the Syrian throne (a circumstance that the Jews were sometimes able to turn to their advantage). Ever since the Romans had done battle with Antiochus the Great (192–189), they too had been keeping an eye on developments in Syria, so that Judas thought it prudent to request their aid. They did not yet, however, choose to deploy their legions.

The Syrians continued to exercise sovereign rights; a pretender to the throne, Alexander Balas, named Jonathan as high priest. Thus a priest from the countryside came to occupy an office previously reserved for the priestly nobility. He made his first appearance as high priest at the Feast of Booths in 153. This marked the beginning of nearly 120 years during which this office was in the hands of the Hasmoneans, making them the religious leaders not only of the Jews in Judea, but also of the Diaspora Jews, however minimal their actual power might have been. Demetrius I nevertheless gave Simon total exemption from paying taxes and thus independence. "In the one hundred and seventieth year [of the Seleucid era], the yoke of the Gentiles was taken from Israel, and the people of Israel began to write in the contracts and agreements: 'In the first year of Simon, the High Priest and commander and sovereign of the Jews'" (I Macc. 13:41-42). The introduction of the new era through the new method for dating announced political independence. Coinage bearing the inscription "High Priest" followed. In May of 142, Simon compelled the Syrian garrison to hand over the citadel. The populace acknowledged his eternal sovereignty—that is, that his descendants would rule after him. In December of 139, an embassy to Rome obtained Simon senatorial recognition.

The internal situation in the now independent state was not yet stable, however. The Hellenists had been decimated and had lost their influence. But the Sadducees, who comprised primarily the upper classes under the high priest and refused to acknowledge any authority beyond the Torah, had to confront the Pharisees, a popular party that constructed a "fence about the law" by means of elaborations based on oral tradition, implementation of strict controls over everyday life and festival observance through detailed legalism. They also recognized the Prophets and Hagiographa as Scripture, and, at least among certain groups, promoted apocalyptic speculation. Separatist groups like the Essenes also sprang up; the Qumran community was probably such a movement. These separatists had probably retreated to escape the bloody clashes of the present; carefully preserving their esoteric way of life, they placed all their hopes in God's intervention at the imminent eschaton.

Jonathan and Simon had already succeeded in expanding the territory of the Jews by conquering such Hellenistic cities as Joppa and Gezer. Now John Hyrcanus (135–104) conquered Samaria and destroyed the sanctuary on Gerizim. He also subjugated portions of Transjordan and, in the south, the Idumeans, whom he forced to accept circumcision. His successor, Aristobulus I, assumed the title of king, but on his coinage continued to style himself "High Priest" of Judah. He undertook a campaign against the Itureans, who lived in Galilee and in regions to the northeast of Galilee, and made Galilee Jewish territory once more. His successor, Alexander Janneus (103–76), continued this policy of conquest with varying success. Some of his coinage continued to bear Hebrew inscriptions, the title "High Priest," and the name of Jonathan; and he was also the first to issue bilingual coinage using the term "King." He was succeeded by his wife Alexandra

(76–67). She granted the Pharisees considerable influence. Her eldest son Hyrcanus became high priest; thus after three quarters of a century the temporal power was once more separated from the spiritual. After the death of Alexandra, the high priest Hyrcanus had a claim to the kingship. His younger brother Aristobulus II, however, defeated the supporters of Hyrcanus near Jericho and compelled Hyrcanus to relinquish even the office of high priest. At this point the Idumean, Antipater, came on the scene. He was the son of the Antipater whom Alexander Janneus had appointed governor of Idumea. Meddling in these dynastic quarrels, he persuaded the Arab prince Aretas to support Hyrcanus. After Hyrcanus came to him for asylum, he laid siege to Aristobulus on the hill of the Temple. Now the Romans intervened. Pompey, who had defeated Mithradates in A.D. 66 and had accepted the submission of Tigranes, sent the legate Scaurus to Syria in the year 65. The latter continued on to Judea, where he received gifts from both Hyrcanus and Aristobulus. In 63, Pompey himself came to Damascus but put off the choice between Hyrcanus and Aristobulus until the conclusion of his imminent campaign against the Nabateans. The supporters of Aristobulus wanted to defend Jerusalem, but the supporters of Hyrcanus opened the gates to Pompey, so that he could take possession without a struggle in the person of the legate Piso. The Temple was stormed on the Day of Atonement (according to Josephus) in the year 63. Pompey entered the holy of holies. He reduced the Jewish territory and entrusted it to the high priest Hyrcanus without giving him the title of king and made him subordinate to Scaurus, the governor of Syria. Judea remained subordinate to the province of Syria until A.D. 69.

Hyrcanus II (63–40) remained high priest. When the Roman civil war brought Caesar to power, a senatorial decree even made him ethnarch with the approval of Rome. Antipater nevertheless increasingly took center stage, and tried to wangle positions of power for his two sons Phasael and Herod. In the fall of 41, Antony made both Hyrcanus and Aristobulus tetrarchs of the Jewish territory and restricted Hyrcanus once more to the office of high priest. A raid by the Parthians brought Hyrcanus into captivity. His ears were cut off, which rendered him unfit to be high priest, and he was replaced by Antigonus (40–35), whom the Parthians installed as high priest and king with the Hebrew name Mattathias. Ventidius, the legate of Antony, drove the Parthians out, but left Antigonus in office. In the meantime (toward the end of 40 B.C.), the Roman Senate had declared Herod king of Judea. In the following year Herod landed in Ptolemais. Not until the spring of 37, however, was he able to lay siege to Jerusalem, which he took after a long and bitter struggle. Antigonus was taken to Antioch by the legate Sosius and beheaded. In the year 35, Herod (37–4) named the Hasmonean Aristobulus II to be high priest, but in the very same year had him drowned in his bath at Jericho. Herod was able to hold on to the kingship thanks to his good relationship with Rome, the adroitness with which he transferred his allegiance from Antony to Octavian, the ruthlessness with which he removed his real or supposed opponents, and the generosity he exhibited even to cities outside his own domain, which the Romans had gradually extended as the years passed. He loved ostentation, had a mania for squandering money on public works, and was devoted to the Hellenistic-Roman way of life, but he could call on the power of Rome for support and remained in favor with Rome until his death. He died in Jericho and was buried in his magnificent fortress Herodium, south of Bethlehem. After his death, his territory was divided among his sons Philip, Herod Antipas, and Archelaus; none of them, however, received the right to style himself king. Philip and Herod Antipas ruled as tetrarchs, the former over the northeast, the latter over Galilee and Perea. Archelaus was appointed ethnarch over Judea, but was exiled to Vienna in Gaul (Vienne). Until A.D. 41, his territory was administered by Roman procurators mostly from the class of *equites*. Pontius Pilate (A.D. 26–36) was one of these procurators. Their administration gave rise to considerable unrest. The first occasion was the census in the year 5, the next the appearance of a certain Judas from Gamala, who, together with a Pharisee named Zadok, founded the Zealot party. The somewhat insensitive Pilate tried to have images of the emperor brought to Jerusalem and only removed them after enraged Jews stormed the official residence of the procurators in Caesarea by the Sea, demanding that this measure be repealed. He enraged the populace even more by dipping into the Temple treasury to build an aqueduct for Jerusalem. He was finally recalled for instigating a bloodbath among the Samaritans because he had feared a rebellion. In A.D. 38 there were violent disturbances in Alexandria, with the Jews who refused to participate in the imperial cult honoring Caligula being the victims. When Caligula demanded that an image of himself be set up in the Jerusalem Temple, all that prevented a rebellion were the delaying tactics of the governor of Syria, Petronius (39–42). Caligula was assassinated in A.D. 41, and the statue was never set up. Now once more a Herodian became king over Judea, Herod Agrippa. In the year 37, Caligula had already granted Herod the tetrarchies of Philip (4–34) and Lysanias (28–37) (who ruled over Aulanitis), together with the title of king. Herod Agrippa had supported the acclamation of Claudius as emperor, and now Claudius added Judea and Samaria to his territories. He took great pains to follow the ancestral customs of the Jews as interpreted by the Pharisees. It was under him that James was martyred. The same fate had been intended for Peter. Outside of Judea he promoted Hellenism, as can be seen from his coinage; the coins he minted for Judea bore no image, while those minted for other regions bore the image of Agrippa or of the emperor. His death in 44 brought all of Palestine under the rule of Roman procurators.

Herod Agrippa had been sensitive to the customs and sensibilities of the Jews; now the Jews found themselves all the more restricted in their views and rights. Cuspius

Fadus, the first of the procurators, demanded that the regalia of the high priest be kept in Roman custody, as in the years between A.D. 6 and 36, and be made available only on festivals. An appeal to the Emperor Claudius succeeded in having this measure repealed. The procurator also had a supposed prophet Theudas ambushed and killed, together with a number of his followers. Under Ventidius Cumanus, the third procurator, there were bloody revolts. Felix aroused hostility through his marriage to Drusilla, an Herodian, and proceeded energetically but somewhat incautiously against the Zealots. This occasioned the appearance of an even more radical group, the *sicarii,* who did not even shrink from assassinating the high priest Jonathan. Fanatics sprang up among the populace and demanded a war of liberation; they quickly gained support. Porcius Festus (60–62) was likewise unable to suppress the *sicarii.* The high priests also had a share in the general collapse. Agrippa II (50–100) played a part, as well. Claudius had bestowed on him the kingdom along the Lebanon, together with supervision of the Temple and the right to appoint high priests. When Gessius Florus (64–66) dipped into the Temple treasury, open rebellion erupted; neither Ananias, the high priest, nor Agrippa, the king, was able to calm the populace.

Jerusalem was divided into two parties. The supporters of the high priest gradually lost ground, for the rebels had occupied the Temple hill and its fortress, the Antonia. Cestius Gallius, the governor of Syria, brought a powerful force to Jerusalem but withdrew after a fruitless attack on the Temple hill. Ambushed near Beth Horon, he was slain while trying to escape. Now even the party favoring peace was ready for battle. At first hostilities were concentrated in Galilee. In the year 67, Vespasian and his son Titus put down the rebellion. John of Giscala fled to Jerusalem with his Zealots; Josephus, who had organized the struggle, was taken captive. The high priests tried to drive the Zealots out of the Temple precincts (which they were holding), but the Zealots called on the Idumeans for help. This marked the beginning of a bitter civil war within the city. Vespasian later laid siege to Jerusalem after conquering the environs. In the year 70 he began his attack upon Jerusalem from the north, finally reducing Jerusalem to a heap of rubble on which a Roman garrison set up its camp. Some *sicarii* under the leadership of Eleazar ben Jairi held out until 73 in the mountain fortress of Masada.

Judea was now administered by consular governors whose official residences were in Caesarea by the Sea. Flavia Neapolis, the modern Nablus, was refounded. A temple of Zeus was built on Mount Gerizim. The Temple in Jerusalem passed out of existence, and the sacrificial cult, without its site, came to an end. The Sadducees had been so decimated in the struggle that they vanished from the stage of history. The Pharisees formed synagogue congregations. Rabbi Johanan ben Zakkai became the head of a learned academy in Jamnia (Jabne). The tribunal the academy established exercised ultimate authority in all religious questions. The Mishnah came into being. In 115, when Trajan (98–117) was emperor, there was a Jewish revolt in Egypt and Cyrene in which both sides fought ferociously. It was not totally put down until the reign of Hadrian (117–138). When this emperor was on the throne, there was a final great revolt in Judea (132–135). Its occasion may have been a tightening up of the castration laws and their extension to circumcision (Spartian). Dio Cassius thinks the revolt was brought about by a plan to found Aelia Capitolina on the ruins of Jerusalem. Simon bar Kosba, exalted by his followers as Simon bar Kochba (Simon the Star) and ridiculed by the Talmud as Simon bar Kozba (Simon the Liar), placed himself at the head of a messianic movement supported by Rabbi Akiba. The governor of Judea, Tineius Rufus, was not able to put down the revolt; troops from other provinces had to intervene also. The final battle flared up at Beth Ter (Qaṣr Yahūd). After a difficult siege, the fortress fell (A.D. 134). Bar Kosba was killed. By the terebinth of Abraham near Hebron the captives were sold into slavery. The colony of

JUDAISM OUTSIDE THE HEBREW CANON

Aelia Capitolina was founded to replace Jerusalem; no Jew was allowed to enter this colony upon penalty of death. The last great revolt of the Jews spelled the end for apocalypticism. Under the leadership of Pharisaic rabbis, Judaism retreated to the Torah and the Torah's interpretation in the Mishnah.

Intellectual Milieu

T. F. Glasson, "Apocalyptic Ideas of Judaism Contemporary with Our Lord," *LondonQHolbR*, XXIX:3 (1960):166–70; M. Noth, "Das Geschichtsverständnis der alttestamentlichen Apokalyptik," *Geschichtsdenken und Geschichtsbild im Mittlelalter*, ed. W. Lammers, 1961, pp. 30–54 (English: "The Understanding of History in Old Testament Apocalyptic," *The Laws of the Pentateuch and Other Essays* [1966], pp. 194–214); L. H. Brockington, *Ideas of Mediation Between God and Man in the Apocrypha*, 1962; H. H. Rowley, *The Relevance of Apocalyptic*, 1947, 2nd ed., rev., 1964; D. S. Russell, *The Method and Message of Jewish Apocalyptic*, Old Testament Library, 1964; R. Meyer, *Tradition und Neuschöpfung im antiken Judentum*, 1965; N. N. Glatzer, *Anfänge des Judentums*, 1966; H. F. Weiss, *Untersuchungen zur Kosmologie des hellenistischen und palästinischen Judentums*, 1966; M. Hengel, *Judentum und Hellenismus*, 1969 (English: *Judaism and Hellenism*, 1974).

It is impossible to find a single common denominator to describe the religious and intellectual milieu of Judaism at the beginning of the fourth century B.C. A mere reference to the territorial fragmentation of the Jews is enough to show why. In the first place, there were the Jews in and around Jerusalem, who, led by Zerubbabel, had settled around the Temple (rebuilt in 516 B.C.) and felt themselves more or less distinct from the Samaritans, who in turn had the political advantage that the Persian governor of all Palestine had his residence in Samaria. Second, there were the Jews living in exile, descendants of those deported by

Nebuchadnezzar in 597, 593, and 586 b.c.; all the evidence suggests that they participated actively in the economic life of their new homeland and found their situation in the Diaspora a constant incentive to cultivating their individuality. There were still other Diaspora Jews in Egypt, presumably because Jewish mercenaries had settled there since the sixth century (Elephantine); with the passage of time, their numbers increased for several reasons but especially because Ptolemy I deported many Jews.

Let us turn to the Jewish heartland. Here the Jews' acceptance of the Law as proclaimed by Ezra furnished the legal basis for a limited special status enjoyed by the Temple community and even more so by the Jews in general; for in promulgating the Law (probably the entire Torah, with the possible exception of minor interpolations), Ezra had acted as a Persian official on the mandate of the great king. By so doing, he had placed every Jew under the obligation of living according to the laws summarized and codified in the Torah. This was an act of goodwill on the part of the Persians to prevent the forced assimilation of the Jews. But the Torah contained more than laws; it also contained promises recorded in narratives and in the history of the past—history guided by God's governance as the Jews, proud of their forefathers and awed by the power of Yahweh in history, had told it over the course of centuries. Of course the account of this history was overgrown with myths and legends; its preservation, however, attested that Yahweh's hand was seen less in the normal cycle of the year, in seedtime and harvest, than in the causation of historical situations. Then it would be assisted by the forces of nature, likewise subject to the creative will of this powerful God, which would reveal their devastating power in catastrophes and their beneficence, as well, in the cycle of the year. Even the Samaritans adopted this Torah, because, by virtue of its origin, it was not only a religious but a political document, providing an opportunity to live according to ancestral laws and customs under Persian protection.

JUDAISM OUTSIDE THE HEBREW CANON

Now it is true that ever since Josiah's reign (621 B.C.) the Jews had been under obligation to a covenant book, the so-called Deuteronomy. When Ezra promulgated the Law, there were added only two new elements: the document that the Jews of Palestine accepted as binding was much more comprehensive, and it was no longer a Judean king but a foreign sovereign who permitted this affirmation of the Law and bound himself by it. Anyone living as a Jew in accordance with these divine ordinances had the rights of a full citizen in the Persian Empire. Since this Law also guaranteed the prerogatives of the priesthood, it is easy to see why the priests in particular adhered to the Torah. The Sadducean party, which came into being towards the end of the second century B.C., opposed any addition to the corpus of sacred scripture, probably because they did not want to provoke any discussion of this privilege enjoyed by the Jews since the time of Ezra. Finally, the Torah was the basis for the interpretation of the Law practiced by the scribes as finally codified in the Mishnah (completed around A.D. 200) and in the Talmud (completed during the fifth century).

But other documents of antiquity had been preserved as well—the writings of the prophets on the one hand, the writings of the wisdom teachers on the other. The words and deeds of the prophets were recorded in narrative books and collections of their sayings. These were handed down and read in private circles. They were recalled and quoted on appropriate occasions. But it was not until the beginning of the second century that the Pharisees succeeded in having these documents officially incorporated into the worship of the synagogue, albeit ranked a step below the Torah. What the prophets said could not always be harmonized with what the Torah said, and the prophets' occasional violent polemic against the cult displeased the priests. The threats and promises spoken by the prophets were given contemporary significance and used in apocalyptic calculations that were not always opportune. At least in the Seleucid and Roman period such

48

interpretations led to many clashes with the foreign powers that ruled Palestine. The prophets' pastoral admonitions, their threats of judgment to come (which people from the time of Haggai and Zechariah onward thought had been fulfilled in the catastrophes of 722 and 586), and their promises (whose fulfillment extensive segments of the population hoped for with varying intensity) pointed beyond the present, recalling on the one hand the glorious era of the Davidic and Solomonic monarchy and opening on the other a gateway to the future through which the faithfulness of Yahweh would produce a wonderful prosperity of eternal duration.

The wisdom literature was bound up more closely with the present, striving to show that prudent conduct with respect to God and man was the way to happiness. In the figure of Job, it presented an exemplary man who succeeded in maintaining his faith in God in the face of all hardships and temptations and therefore received God's reward. In the poetry of the Psalms the praise of God, as well as lamentation over God's distance in the midst of sickness and disaster, resounded. The religious poetry seems to have been in the hands of laymen who banded together to form guilds of singers and sought acceptance into the circle of Levites.

The Persian period, little affected by external convulsions (cf. Zech. 1:11ff.), offered favorable circumstances for the collection and expansion of ancient traditions and the cultivation of traditional literary forms, both in Palestine and in the Mesopotamian Diaspora, which had come into being through the deportations of the eighth and sixth centuries. The Elephantine documents and scattered references in the Prophets (e.g., Jer. 43:7ff.; 44:1; 46:14) furnish what little information we have about the Egyptian Diaspora. Here, too, the Diaspora situation permitted a community life that, if not unmolested, was at least bearable, as is shown by the construction of a sanctuary at Jeb (Elephantine). Here, too, we can see that the dangers to which the purity of the cult of Yahweh was exposed (evident from the narratives of Elijah and Elisha and from the threats of Hosea and Jeremiah) were not escaped at Jeb, where Anatyahu and Ashim-Bethel were worshiped alongside Yahweh; it is significant that, despite Ezekiel 8:11 ff., Egyptian influence shows itself at most in the divine triad, although the gods themselves were of Israelite/Canaanite origin. The Persian policy of toleration made it all the more easy to maintain Jewish identity. Greater emphasis on the God of heaven as well as the development of Satan (who had played the role of accuser in the court of Yahweh) into an enemy of Yahweh, a process that begins in Job and becomes manifest in the Testaments of the Twelve Patriarchs and the Qumran documents may have been encouraged by the religion of Zoroaster. Greater emphasis on an eschatological judgment associated with a resurrection of the dead was probably also strongly stimulated by the Persian religion, thus bringing to flower elements that had been embryonically present. It was this possibility of discovering related themes in the religion of the Persians, making it possible to seek a rapprochement with the ruling powers, that lessened the temptation of Babylonian religion for the exiles. Its influence remained confined to those circles that had slipped into magic and sorcery.

The peace and contentment of the Persian Empire had provided an opportunity for Judaism to develop intellectually and religiously. When the invasion of Alexander shattered this peace, new ideas of Greek mythology and philosophy, indeed of Greek civilization in general, flooded into the world of the Near East. How extensive their influence was can be seen in the acceptance of Hellenistic institutions like theaters and stadiums by both the high priests and the ruling classes. Some Jews even refused circumcision, the sign of the covenant, or sought to disguise the fact that it had been performed. But it was impossible to open the doors to the outward manifestations of Western civilization without at the same time encountering the ideology behind them and being forced to come to terms with it. One way to do this was to attempt to correlate these new ideas as much as possible with traditional views, as is done, for example, in the Wisdom of Solomon and later by Philo of Alexandria. It was also possible, however, to recognize the foreign spirit as being incompatible with traditional Yahwism and thus to strive to maintain pure religion, as did the Maccabees. Finally, it was possible to withdraw into conventicles and cultivate a private sanctity mingled with many special doctrines. This was what happened at Qumran, as is evidenced by the religious documents and related literature produced there. The problem of what was to become of the nation as a whole could be approached by the specialized groups in two ways: the nation could be rigorously repudiated as a mass of perdition, or the people could be viewed as brothers who would be brought to the group when the day of salvation dawned and then be educated so that they could be God's people. Other groups were wont to take refuge in apocalyptic fantasies, keeping their sights trained on the distant goal of a restored world in the midst of daily life and its temptations.

Significant remnants of this wealth of ideas and configurations were preserved by the agency of Christianity, especially in fringe areas outside the church of the empire. Most recently the important original texts from Qumran have furnished additional material. This variety came to an end by the close of the second century c.e., when Judaism, faced with the challenge of Christianity, committed itself to its central document, the Torah, and the group of sacred writings that, rightly or wrongly, could be traced back to the period between Moses and Ezra. The writings that Judaism excluded at this time constitute the Apocrypha and pseudepigrapha, the subject matter of this introduction.

II. THE APOCRYPHA

Judith

Text: Greek—Swete, II:781–814; Rahlfs, I:973–1002; Brooke-McLean, III:1, 43–84. Latin—*Vulgata,* I:691–711; *Biblia Sacra,* VII:211–80; Fritzsche-Grimm (O. F. Fritsche). Translations: Charles (A. E. Cowley), I:242–67; Kautzsch (M. Löhr), I:147–64; Clamer-B (L. Soubigou), 1949; Monserrat-B (M. M. Estradé and B. M. Girbau), 1960; Echter-B (F. Stummer), 1950; Herder-B (H. Bückers), 1953; Jerusalem-B (A. Barucq), 2nd ed., 1959; Kahana (M. Simon), 2nd ed., 1956; SaBi (G. Priero), 1959. Commentaries: A. Miller, (*HS*), 1940; J. Grintz, ספר יהודית, 1957; A. Scholz, *Commentar über das Buch Judith und über Bel und Drache,* 2nd ed., 1896; A. Deprez, "Le livre de Judith," *Évangile,* XLVII (1962):5–69; S. Grzybek, S. Baksik, and S. Grzybek, *Ksiega Tobiasza; Ksiega Judyty; Ksiega Estery,* Pismo Sw. Starego Testamentu, 6:1-3, 1963.

Monographs: J. Alonso Díaz, *Lo desconcertante en el libro de Judith,* 1961; E. Haag, "Die besondere literarische Art des Buches Judith und seine theologische Bedeutung," *TriererThz,* LXXI (1962):288–301; *idem,* "Studien zum Buche Judith, *TriererThSt,* 1963; P. W. Skehan, "The Hand of Judith," *CBQ,* XXV (1963):94–110; E. Haag, "Der Widersacher Gottes nach dem Buch Judith," *BiKi,* XIX:2 (1964), pp. 28–42; J. C. Greenfield, "מסע נבוכדנאצר בספר יהודית [Nebuchadnezzar's Campaign in the Book of Judith]," *Yediot,* XXVIII (1964):204–8; R. Criado, "Judit, Libro de," *EncBib,* IV (1965):768–72; I. Moutsoulas, " Ἰουδίθ," *Thresk EthEnk,* VI (1965):941–43; A. M.

Dubarle, "Judith", Analecta biblica, 24, 1966; *idem*, "Judith (Livre de)," *Catholicisme*, VII, 1966.

BHH, II:912 (B. M. Metzger); *RGG*, III:1000–1001 (E. Jenny—W. Werbeck); Eissfeldt, pp. 793–96, 1021 (English: 585–87, 771) *IDB*, II:1023–26 (P. Winter).

Text

That the book of Judith goes back to a Hebrew original is shown, for example, by its use of parataxis and its lack of such common Greek particles as μέν, δέ, ἄρα, etc. Only the Greek text has been preserved and that, in three versions: (1) the version of Septuagint codices B and A—Sinaiticus often agrees with the latter; (2) the Lucianic recension found in codices 19 and 108; and (3) codex 58, with which the Old Latin and Syriac agree.

Derivative translations besides the Old Latin comprise two almost literal Syriac ones—the Peshitta translation and the Hexaplaric translation by Paul of Tella produced in Alexandria around 616.

As the basis for his Vulgate translation, Jerome used an Aramaic text that exhibits a few discrepancies. Therefore, it cannot derive immediately from the lost Hebrew original. Short Hebrew translations going back to an Aramaic text of the eleventh century are known through editions printed in 1519 and 1544 (Gaster). According to A. M. Dubarle, these derive from an ancient tradition, now lost, that is related to the Old Latin and is independent of both the Septuagint and Vulgate. To date, texts of the book of Judith have not been found at Qumran.

Contents

The narrative focuses on an heroic act on the part of Judith to deliver Bethulia, a city besieged by Holofernes, one of Nebuchadnezzar's generals. The book is organized as follows: In chapters 1:1–3:9, Nebuchadnezzar wages war against the Medes without support from the west. Having defeated the Medes, he determines to punish the west and sends forth his armies. All the west falls before him except

53

the Jews, who are represented by the city of Bethulia. In 3:1–7:32, Holofernes marches against the Jews. Achior, leader of the Ammonites, instructs him about the history of the Jews and their relationship with God. Holofernes is enraged at Achior and hands him over to the Jews of Bethulia, while laying siege to the city by surrounding it and cutting off its water supply. The Jews are terrified and consider surrendering the city if God does not help them within five days. In 8:1–14:19, Judith decides to go into the camp of Holofernes with her maid; Holofernes asks her to stay; she slays him and brings his head back to the people of Bethulia. In 15:1–16:29, the Assyrians are defeated, Judith sings a song of praise, is honored by her fellow townspeople and the inhabitants of Jerusalem, and dies at the age of 105, having bequeathed her property and given her maidservant her freedom.

Literary Criticism

The book of Judith turns out to be a single unit, even to the Song of Judith. Its first section (16:2-13) is a victory paean modeled on the Song of Deborah that emphasizes the part played by Judith. The second section (16:14-18) is a hymn praising God for his omnipotence as exhibited in creation and in history. This places Judith's deed in its proper perspective: it is one small episode in the history of God's mighty acts.

Judith is a single complete narrative; nothing has been lost. It begins with an exposition like that of Genesis 14 and thus places the story within the grand sweep of history. It ends, like Job, with the death of the heroine.

Historicity

Judith purports to be an event in the great conflict between a world power, symbolized by Nebuchadnezzar, and the Jewish community, represented by the city of Bethulia. Contrary to the fact of history, Nebuchadnezzar is king of Assyria and has his residence in Nineveh. The Temple is standing, and the deportees have just returned from captivity in Babylonia. The general Holofernes has a Persian name. This Holofernes is known to have been a general under Artaxerxes III Ochus, who led a campaign against Egypt. The eunuch Bagoas, who advises Holofernes in the Book of Judith, is mentioned as an adviser of Artaxerxes (*Diodorus Siculus* xvi. 471; xxi. 9). Either the author saw in the Persian king an incarnation of Nebuchadnezzar and in his rule a rebirth of the Assyrian Empire (which would mean that he made use of pseudonyms to describe an episode that took place under Artaxerxes III on the periphery of Holofernes' Egyptian campaign), or he made the story up out of whole cloth. The latter is more probable, since the historical Holofernes returned to his Cappadocian satrapy after the Egyptian campaign, having survived the battle.

Genre

Judith, then, turns out to be a narrative based on literary invention; it belongs with Tobit, Ruth, and Esther. A world power confronts the Jewish community, which God helps not through the power of his armies and the effectiveness of their weapons, but through an unarmed woman, who beheads the foe with his own sword just as Jael slays Sisera with a hammer and David kills Goliath. The author draws on these and other heroic deeds in order that his story, set in the recent past, may give those who share his faith courage to endure oppression and trust that God will help them, just as Judith and Deborah inspired courage in their contemporaries.

Date and Authorship

Since Holofernes and Bagoas probably belong to the period of Artaxerxes III, the narrative can probably not be dated earlier than toward the end of the Persian period. The mention of wreaths (3:7) makes it more likely that the author wrote his edifying tale during the Hellenistic period after 300 B.C., albeit there is no further evidence of Hellenistic influence. Since his list of possible transgressions does not include apostasy, but only indifference to the dietary laws and Temple tax, the period of Antiochus IV Epiphanes can hardly be considered.

The author is a Jew faithful to the Law; he puts all his faith and confidence in Yahweh's omnipotence, not in human strength.

Religious Significance

The book thinks of Yahweh as creator and as one who exercises his power in history. He uses affliction to test his people, but as long as they remain faithful to the Law he will not give them over to their enemies. Man's duty is therefore to obey the Law punctiliously, to appeal to God's compassion in affliction by prayer and fasting, and to await his help despite all outward appearances that the situation is hopeless. But whoever—like Judith—is called upon by God to take action should do so with resourcefulness and vigor.

Wisdom of Solomon

Text: Greek—Swete, II:604–43; Rahlfs, II:345–76; LXX Gott., XII:1. Latin—*Vulgata*, II:1003–28; *Biblia Sacra*, XII:5–104; Fritzsche-Grimm (W. Grimm).

Translations: Charles (S. Holmes), I:518–68; Kautzsch (K. Siegfried), I:476–507; Echter-B (J. Fischer), 1950; Herder-B (E. Kalt), 1938; Jerusalem-B (E. Osty), 2nd ed., 1957; Kahana (M. Stein), 2nd ed., 1956.

Commentaries: A. Drubbel (BOuT), 1957; P. Heinisch (EH), 1912; F. Feldmann (*HS*), 1926; J. Reider (*JewApocrLit*), 1957; J. Fichtner (HAT, II:6), 1938; J. Oberski, *Komentar knijige Mudrosti*, 1964.

Monographs: A. Atkins, "Four Ancient Reviews of the Wisdom of Solomon," *LifeSpir*, XVII (1962/63): 505–13; D. Gill, "The Greek Sources of Wisdom XII:3–7," *VT*, XV (1965):383–86; J. B. Bauer, "Drei Cruces," *BZ*, IX (1965):376–80; R. E. Murphy, "Sabiduría, Libro de la," *EncBib*, VI (1965):301–7; J. M. Reese, "Plan and

Structure in the Book of Wisdom," *CBQ*, XXVII (1965):381–83, 391–99; A. G. Wright, "The Structure of Wisd. 11–19," *CBQ*, XXVII (1965):28–34; F. Zimmermann, "The Book of Wisdom: Its Language and Character," *JQR*, NS LVII (1966):7, 1–27, 101–35; A. G. Wright, "Numerical Patterns in the Book of Wisdom," *CBQ*, XXIX (1967):165–84, 524–38; *idem*, "The Structure of the Book of Wisdom," *Bibl*, XLVIII (1967):165–84; F. Festorazzi, "La Sapienza e la Storia della Salvezza," *RB*, XV (1967):151–62; C. Romaniuk, "La traducteur grec du livre de Jésus ben Sira n'est-il pas l'auteur du livre de la sagesse?" *RB*, XV (1967):163–70; *idem*, "More about the Author of the Book of Wisdom," *RB*, XV (1967):543–45; G. Scarpat, "Ancora sull' Autore del Libro della Sapienza," *RB*, XV (1967):171–98; F. Ricken, "Gab es eine hellenistische Vorlage für Weish 13-15?" *Bib*, XLIX (1968):54–86; C. Romaniuk, "Liber Sapientiae qua lingua ubi scriptus sit," *VD*, XLVI (1968):175–80; A. M. Dubarle, "Où en est l'étude de la littérature sapientielle?" *ETL*, XLIV (1968):407–19; W. Baars, "Ein neugefundenes Bruchstück aus der syrischen Bibelrevision des Jakob von Edessa," *VT*, XVIII (1968):548–54.

BHH, III:2158–59 (L. Pap); *RGG*, V:1343–45 (J. Fichtner, W. Werbeck); Eissfeldt, pp. 812–16, 1022 (English: pp. 600–603, 772–73); *IDB*, IV:861–63 (M. Hadas).

Text

The text of the Wisdom of Solomon has been preserved in Greek. Many scholars maintain the possibility of a Hebrew original for the first six chapters, but there is no real evidence for a Hebrew text despite the parallelism and the echoes of Hebrew diction. The hypothesis of intimate familiarity with the LXX is sufficient to explain the impression these chapters give of having been translated from Hebrew. Jerome knows nothing of any Hebrew text. The best Greek text is preserved in B. The other uncials record only a few variants. At Khirbet Mird there have been found fragments of the Greek text; these have not yet been published. Jerome adopts the text of the Old Latin translation, originating in North Africa. There is a Syriac translation that is relatively free and occasionally erroneous. The Armenian version is very literal and of some value for textual criticism.

Contents

The purpose of the book is to lead men to true wisdom and thereby to a life that will be pleasing to Yahweh. It is divided into three sections. The first, 1:1–6:1, shows that wisdom is granted only to the righteous man; despite the persecution of the godless, a glorious destiny awaits him because God will give him immortality. The second section, 6:2–9:19, contains King Solomon's admonition to the kings to seek after wisdom and tells how wisdom was granted him upon his petition and subsequently became his constant companion. The third, 10:1–19:21, recounts the actions God has taken in history to deliver his people and punish their foes.

Literary Criticism

Only in 3:11a and at the beginning of chapter 6 does the book contain proverbs (māšāl). The remainder of the book consists of wisdom discourses. The first chapters exhibit a further development of the style worked out in Proverbs 1:1–9:18; chapter 3 occasionally lapses into prose and takes on the form of a treatise. As a consequence, genres are found that are not associated with wisdom literature: we find (to quote Fichtner) "admonitions (1:1ff.; 6:1ff.), hymnic motifs (11:21ff.; 12:12ff.), prayer (9:1-19), praise of wisdom (6:12ff.; 8:2ff.), discourses (2:1ff.; 5:2ff.), accounts of judgment (5:15ff.; 11–19), debates (11:15ff.; chaps. 13ff.), historical analyses (chaps. 10ff., 16–19), and Greek forms such as sorites (6:17ff.), syncrisis (chaps. 11:16–19), definition (17:11), and enumeration (7:22ff.; 7:16ff.)."

Authorship

All the evidence suggests that the author of Wisdom was an Egyptian Jew, presumably from Alexandria, not totally hostile to Hellenistic influences. It must be recognized, however, that he changed his mind, since the third section differs from the first two in its viewpoints on many questions; these differences require more discussion. But there are so many similarities that one must either assume that two hypothetical authors living in very nearly the same period shared many common attitudes, or, more probably, that a single author was influenced by different ideas in two different periods of his life. Jerome considered Philo to be the author, albeit without justification, since Wisdom contains no trace of Philo's allegorizing method. We probably should conclude therefore that the author was an unknown Alexandrian Jew of the first century B.C. The dating derives from the author's use of Daniel, Enoch, and Tobit and from his mention of a spontaneous ruler cult and unrestrained oppression of devout Jews on the part of apostates.

Teaching and Religious Significance

The author is convinced that God is the almighty creator, preserver, judge, and lord of the universe which he through wisdom made good and beneficent. Nothing can remain hidden from his knowledge, so that he judges even our thoughts. God aids the devout in all their tribulation. Even though he brings many of them to an early death in order to preserve them from an even worse fate, their lives are fulfilled because they receive the crown of immortality. God has been the lord of history since the very beginning—since Adam—as is specifically documented by the exodus from Egypt and the journey of the Israelites through the desert. The wise man is the devout man. Wisdom brings acceptance by others and is the key to receiving esteem. It is folly to deny God and attack the devout, for the godless man will perish.

These ideas have their roots in the wisdom of the Old

Testament, but they have undergone further development and have been augmented by Hellenistic ideas such as the concept of immortality or the notion that a good soul comes in a perfect body. Wisdom, too, can be elaborated after the manner of Stoic philosophy; but it remains almost totally within the bounds of the proverbial wisdom of the Old Testament. The author allows Hellenistic ideas to expand his horizons but also seeks to reconcile them with the biblical basis of his faith.

Tobit

Text: Greek—Swete, II:815–48; Rahlfs, I:1002–39; Brooke-McLean, III:84–122. Latin—*Vulgata*, I:676–90; *Biblia Sacra*, VIII:157–209; Fritzsche-Grimm (O. F. Fritzsche).

Translations: Charles (D. C. Simpson), I:174–241; Kautzsch (M. Löhr), I:135–47; Clamer-B (A. Clamer), 1949; Echter-B (F. Stummer), 1950; Jersualem-B (P. Pautrel), 2nd ed., 1957; Kahana (B. Heller), 2nd ed., 1956; Montserrat-B (M. M. Estradé and B. M. Girbau), 1960; Herder-B (H. Bückers), 1953.

Commentaries: M. Schumpp (EH), 1933; A. Miller (*HS*), 1940; F. Zimmermann, *The Book of Tobit*, 1958; S. Grzybek, S. Baksik, and S. Grzybek, *Ksiega Tobiasza–Ksiega Judyty–Ksiega Estery*, 1963; N. Poulssen, *Tobit*, 1968.

Monographs: E. C. Dell'Oca, "El Libro de Tobit," *RBiCalz*, XXII (1960):214–17; T. Maertens, *Biblia y vida, Tobia*, La Biblia paso a paso, 1960; G. Priero, "Cetera salierunt (Tob. 6:6)," *PalCl*, XL (1961):920–92; J. M. Grintz, "הספרות העברית כבתקופת פרס," *Sefer H. Albeck* (1963), pp. 123–51; L. Arnaldich, "Tobit, Libro de," *EncBib*, VI (1965):1038–41; H. Jansen, "Die Hochzeitsriten im Tobitbuche," *Temenos*, I (1965):142–49; J. T. Milik, "La patrie de Tobie," *RB*, LXXVIII (1966):522–30; W. von Soden, "Fischgalle als Heilmittel für die Augen," *AfO*, XXI (1966):81–82; K. Koch, "Der Schatz im Himmel," *Festschrift H. Thielicke* (1968), pp. 47–60.

BHH, III:1998–99 (B. M. Metzger); *RGG,* VI:907 (R. Meyer; W. Werbeck); Eissfeldt, pp. 790–93 (English, p. 583); *IDB,* IV:658–62 (A. Wikgren).

Text

The book is preserved in three Greek recensions: (1) a longer recension found in Sinaiticus, which exhibits only two major gaps (4:6*b*-19*a* and 13:6*b*-10*a*); (2) a slightly abbreviated and edited recension in Alexandrinus and Vaticanus; and (3) a recension found in minuscules 44, 106, and 107, which exhibits a unique text in 6:7-13:8 and elsewhere agrees with the second recension. The Old Latin version basically follows Sinaiticus. Jerome translated the Vulgate from an Aramaic manuscript that was translated orally into Hebrew for him; it diverges from the other versions, especially at the beginning. Luther follows the Vulgate. The Syriac translation, probably done by Paul of Tella, follows Vaticanus. Another Syriac translation is closely related to the third Greek recension. There are several medieval Hebrew and Aramaic translations which bear witness to the popularity of the story of Tobit among the Jews during the Middle Ages. According to G. Dalman, one Aramaic translation derives from the seventh century. Fragments of one Hebrew and two Aramaic manuscripts have recently been found at Qumran; unfortunately they do not settle the ancient debate over whether the Greek text is based on a Hebrew or Aramaic original. They are closely related to Sinaiticus. It seems reasonable to conclude that the book was initially written in Aramaic and very soon afterwards translated into Hebrew, with the Hebrew version furnishing the basis for the Greek translation. The hypothesis of a Hebrew original retaining a few Aramaisms best explains the word order and several other peculiarities of the Greek translation.

Contents

Tobit, of the tribe of Naphtali, tells how he, his wife, and his son Tobias were deported to Nineveh. Tobit had always upheld strict observance of the Law; in particular he endeavored to bury those of his faith and even forewent a festival dinner to carry out this obligation in the face of a prohibition by the Assyrian authorities. One night when he is sleeping outdoors after such a deed, droppings from a swallow fall into his eyes, and he is blinded (1:3–3:6). At the same time in Ecbatana, Sara, the daughter of Raguel, is reproached by her maid, who accuses her of having brought about the death of each of her seven husbands on their wedding night. In response to their prayers, God sends his angel Raphael to assist both Tobit and Sara (3:7-17). Tobit decides to dispatch his son Tobias to Media to collect a sum of money he had deposited with Gabael there. Raphael, posing as a kinsman, is prepared to accompany Tobias (4:1–5:22). Tobias' companion instructs him to catch a fish and keep its gall, liver, and heart as medicine. At the same time, Raphael indicates that Sara is meant to be Tobias' bride (6:1-22). Upon arriving in Ecbatana, Tobias immediately requests the hand of his cousin Sara. Thanks to the liver and heart of the fish, which Tobias burns, the wedding night passes without incident, since the smoke renders the demon Asmodaeus impotent. Fourteen days of celebration follow, during which Raphael/Azariah collects the money from Gabael (7:1–9:12). In Nineveh, meanwhile, Tobit and Hannah have grown alarmed because the travelers are so long in returning. Finally, amid great rejoicing, Tobias arrives with Sara and Raphael. Tobias uses the gall of the fish to heal his father's blindness. A joyous banquet ensues (10:1–11:20), and Raphael reveals his identity (12:1-22). Chapter 13 contains a hymn of Tobit. The book concludes with chapter 14, which contains Tobit's final words and an account of his death.

Literary Criticism

Literary criticism raises only one problem: do we not find the original conclusion of the narrative in the banquet at the end of chapter 12, thus making it likely that the hymn in chapter 13 and the conclusion in chapter 14 are mere appendices? This must be considered a possible conclusion, although the style of chapter 14 does not differ from that found in the rest of the book. If chapters 13 and 14 had already been appended in the Aramaic original or the Hebrew translation, the uniformity of style would not be surprising.

Place and Date

The book is an edifying legend. Its only historical value is that it gives evidence of a Judaism that allows magical practices to exist side by side with strict observance of the Law. The author's unfamiliarity with the geography of eastern Mesopotamia and his vague ideas about circumstances in Assyria hardly make it possible to date the narrative at the beginning of the seventh century B.C. It must instead be dated at around 200 B.C.; its author may have lived in Egypt or, more likely, western Syria.

Genres and Motifs

The legendary narrative has incorporated wisdom proverbs both for what Tobit supposes to be his last words in 4:6-20 and for Raphael's speech in 12:8-10. In addition, 13:2-22 interpolates a hymn to Yahweh's omnipotence and righteousness in the past, present, and future. Blessings and prayers enliven the narrative in the fashion common since the Yahwist.

What is abnormal is the extent to which the book incorporates fairy-tale motifs and foreign material. It draws on the story of Ahikar by incorporating this government official and representative of wisdom genealogically and by placing elements from his story in the course of the narrative. Tobit is based on a particular form of the fable of the grateful dead, as the Tractate of Khôns shows. Motifs associated with the slaying of a dragon are also found; in this fable the meaningless dog in the book of Tobit plays a role. There are also traces of a healer story. Whether the author combined these materials himself or found them already linked through oral tradition can no longer be determined.

Theological Significance

The narrative reveals a Judaism typified by faithful fulfillment of the Law. The voluntarily accepted obligation not to allow a corpse to remain unburied overnight, even when this runs counter to the Gentile sovereign, plays an important role. Fasting and prayer are considered ways of influencing God. The devout man bears the strokes of fortune like Job. When the cup of testing is filled to the brim, God will intervene—under certain circumstances, miraculously. He can make use of his angels (who can appear in human form but do not need human sustenance) to aid men by word and deed. Belief in angels is accompanied by belief in demons and in demons' hostile intervention in human destiny. Mysterious powers of strange medicines such as the liver, heart, and gall of a fish serve to overcome these demons. These are analogous to the popular remedies still recommended in the tractate "Sabbath" of the Babylonian Talmud: in other words, magic turns out to be beneficent; it is even suggested by one of God's angels and is therefore legitimate for an Israelite.

Jesus Sirach (Ecclesiasticus)

Text: Greek—Swete, II:644–754; Rahlfs, II:377–471; LXX Gott., XII:2; Latin—*Vulgata*, II:1029–95; *Biblia Sacra*, XII:105–375; Hebrew—R. Smend, *Die Weisheit des Jesus Sirach, hebräisch und deutsch*, 1906; M. H. Segal, ספר בן סירא השלם, 2nd. ed., 1959; Y. Yadin, *The Ben Sira Scroll from Masada*, 1965; M. Baillet, J. T. Milik, and R. de Vaux, *Les 'Petites Grottes' de Qumran (Discoveries in the Judaean Desert of Jordan 3)*, 1962 (pl. 15, pp. 75–77); Fritzsche-Grimm (O. F. Fritzsche).

Translations: Charles (G. H. Box and W. O. E. Oesterley), I:268–517; Kautzsch (V. Ryssel), I:230–475; Echter-B (V. Hamp), 1951; Herder-B (Schilling), 1956;

Jerusalem-B (H. Duesberg and P. Auvray), 1958; Kahana (A. Kahana), 2nd ed., 1956; E. S. Hartum, (ספרים חיצונים) בן סירא, 1963.

Commentaries: J. Knabenbauer (CSS), 1902; N. Peters (EH), 1913; A. Eberharter (*HS*), 1925; P. Volz (SAT), 1921; B. Vawter, *The Book of Sirach* (Pamphlet Bible Series), 1962; H. Duesberg and I. Fransen, "Ecclesiastico" (*La Santa Bibbia*, a cura di S. Carofalo, AT sotto la direzione di G. Rinaldi), 1966; A. van den Bron, *Wijsheid van Jesus Sirach (Ecclesiasticus)*, 1968.

Monographs: J. Ziegler, *Die Münchener griechische Sirach-Handschrift 493; ihre textgeschichtliche Bedeutung und erstmalige Edition durch den Augsburger Humanisten David Hoeschel (1604)* (SAM, 1962:4); L. Scazzocchio, "Eccli, Tobit, Sap. di Salomone alla luce dei testi di Qumran," *RStO*, XXXVII (1962):199–209; A. A. Di Lella, *A Text-Critical and Historical Study of the Hebrew Manuscripts of Sirach*, 1962; idem, "Authenticity of the Geniza Fragments of Sirach," *Biblica*, XLIV (1963):23–30; M. Fang Che-Yong, "De discrepantiis inter textum graecum et hebraicum libri Sira," dissertation, Pontifical Biblical Institute, 1963; idem, "Usus nominis divini in Sirach," *VD*, XLII (1964):155–68; idem, *Quaestiones theologicae selectae Libri Sirach ex comparatione textus graeci et hebraici ortae*, 1963; W. Fuss, "Tradition und Komposition im Buche Jesus Sirach," dissertation, Tübingen, 1963; J. Ziegler, "Die Vokabel-Varianten der O-Rezension im griechischen Sirach," *Hebrew and Semitic Studies Presented to G. R. Driver*, 1963; P. W. Skehan, "Didache 1:6 and Sir 12:1," *Bib*, XLIV (1963):533–36; R. E. Murphy, "Eclesiastico," *EncBib*, II (1965):1056–58; R. Pautrel, "Ben Sira et le Stoicisme," *RecSR*, LI (1963):535–49; M. H. Segal, "ספר בן־סירא בקומרן," *Tarbits*, XXXIII (1963/64):243–46; A. Sisti, "Riflessi dell'epoca premaccabaica nell'Ecclesiastico," *RBiblt*, XII (1964):215–56; J. Ziegler, "Ursprüngliche Lesarten im griechischen Sirach," *Mélanges Eugène Tisserant*, I (1964):215–56; A. A. Di Lella, "The Recently Identified Leaves of Sirach in Hebrew," *Bib*, XLV (1964):153–67; J.

JUDAISM OUTSIDE THE HEBREW CANON

Ziegler, "Zwei Beiträge zu Sirach," *BZ*, VIII (1964):277–84; A. M. Habermann, "עיונים בספר בן־סירא," *Sefer M. H. Segal*, (1964): 296–99; H. P. Rüger, *Text und Textform; Untersuchungen zur Textgeschichte und Textkritik der hebräischen Sirachfragmente aus der Kairoer Geniza*, Habilitationsschrift, Tübingen, 1965/66; also in BZAW 112 (1970); A. A. Di Lella, *The Hebrew Text of Sirach*, 1966; J. T. Milik, "Un fragment mal placé dans l'édition du Siracide de Masada," *Bibl*, XLVII (1966):425–26; C. Romaniuk, "Le traducteur grec du livre de Jésus ben Sira n'est-il pas l'auteur du livre de la sagesse?" *RB*, XV (1967):163–70; J. M. Baumgarten, "Some Notes on the Ben Sira Scroll from Masada," *JQR*, LVIII (1967/68):323–27; A. M. Dubarle, "Où en est l'étude de la littérature sapientielle?" *ETL*, XLIV (1968):407–19; P. W. Skehan, "Sirach 40:11-17," *CBQ*, XXX (1968):570–72; M. Delcor, "Le texte hébreu du Cantique de Siracide LI 13 et ss. et les anciennes versions," *Textus*, VI (1968): 27–47.

BHH, III:1809–10 (P. Dalbert); *RGG*, III:653–55 (E. Jenni, W. Werbeck); Eissfeldt, pp. 807–12, 1022 (English: 595–99, 772); *IDB*, II:13–21 (T. A. Burkill).

Text

The end of the prologue of the Book of Sirach (in Greek "The Wisdom of Jesus, Son of Sirach") states that it was translated from Hebrew into Greek. This Hebrew Sirach was familiar to Jerome (340/50–420) and was quoted by Maimonides (1135–1204). Since 1896, fragments of five manuscripts from the Cairo Genizah have come to light. These contain a good two-thirds of the Hebrew text:

Ms. A: 2:18*d;* 3:6*a*–16:26*b;* 23:16-17; 27:5-6;

Ms. B: 30:11–36(33):3; 32(35):11–38:27*b;* 39:15*c*–51:30;

Ms. C: 4:23*b*, 30–31; 5:4-7, 9–13; 6:18*b*, 19, 28, 35; 7:1-2, 4, 6*ab*, 17, 20–21, 23–25; 8:31*b;* 19:2*a*, 3*b;* 20:5-7, 13; 25:8, 13, 17–22, 23*cd*, 24; 26:1-2*a;* 36:24*a;* 37:19, 22, 24, 26;

Ms. D: 36:29–38:1a;

Ms. E: 32(35):16–33(30):32; 34:1.

These manuscripts represent two recensions, the shorter of which probably stands closer to the original. While these manuscripts date from the eleventh and twelfth centuries, fragments of the text of 6:20-31 have been found in Cave 2 at Qumran; as far as is known, the Qumran text agrees with that of Cairo. In addition, a manuscript from the first third of the first century B.C. discovered at Masada contains chapters 39–43 (with lacunae); the text is arranged as poetry, in stichs. The Greek translation of the shorter recension is contained in the uncials B, Sinaiticus, A, and various minuscules, while minuscule 248 and others draw on the longer Hebrew recension.

The Greek manuscripts derive from an archetype in which the order of 30:25–33:13a and 33:13b–36:16a has been reversed. The Syriac translation was made directly from the Hebrew text, although it occasionally exhibits the influence of the Greek version—probably because it was later corrected to agree with the Greek translation. The Old Latin version was translated from the Greek and adopted by Jerome. It therefore contains valuable readings. Paul of Tella produced a second Syriac translation, the Syrohexapla, which sometimes preserves good readings. There are further daughter translations of the Greek text into Sahidic, Ethiopic, Armenian, Slavonic, and Arabic.

Title

The Hebrew title of the book has not been preserved. On the evidence of 50:27, it was probably מוסר שכל ומושל אופנים לשמעון בן ישוע בן אלעזר בן סירא, or perhaps more briefly, משלי י׳, a form suggested by Jerome and later rabbinic citations. The Greek title of the book is *Sophía*, "Wisdom." Rufinus explains the Latin title *Ecclesiasticus* as meaning that the book is "churchly," which is most unlikely. The Latin term is probably an expansion of *Ecclesiastes*, the "Preacher," which may refer to Solomon.

Contents

The book begins with a prologue that is not accounted for in the numbering of the chapters. This prologue is followed by wisdom proverbs in *mashal* form; there is no obvious organizing principle, but the proverbs are grouped according to their subject matter. Often a particular theme will be thoroughly discussed by means of a sequence of proverbs treating various aspects of it. The eulogy of the fathers in chapters 43–50 constitutes a special section, which culminates in the glorification of the high priest Simon, son of Onias. The book concludes in chapter 51 with a prayer; prayers have also been interpolated in chapters 22:25–23:6 and 36:1-19.

Author and Date

Jesus ben Eleazar ben Sira was probably a Jew living in Jerusalem. In his way of thinking, he resembles the later Sadducees. The focal point of his reflections is wisdom instruction guided by the Law; but despite his esteem for the priesthood and the cult, he is not cultically motivated. Wisdom and cultic piety are joined in the person of the author, but not in his thought. He says nothing about any resurrection of the dead and nothing at all about the immortality of the soul, which plays a role in the Wisdom of Solomon through Hellenistic influence. That the grandson translates the book in Egypt represents a clear rejection of the Hellenistic ideas that had certainly infiltrated Judaism by this time.

Jesus ben Sira wrote his book in Jerusalem around 190 B.C., presumably when an old man. There is no hint of persecution by Antiochus Epiphanes and nothing at all mentioned about the Maccabean uprising. The high priest Simon who is extolled was probably Simon II, during whose lifetime the work was written. According to the prologue, the grandson went to Egypt in the thirty-eighth year "under Euergetes the king"; this refers to Ptolemy VII Euergetes (170–116 B.C.), so the translation was probably made after 132 B.C.

Genre

The Book of Jesus Sirach is an example of wisdom literature and is closely related to the later portions of the canonical book of Proverbs. It contains sixteen hundred two-line verses. These are organized in small groups, each group dealing with a particular theme.

Religious Content

Sirach recognizes the God of Israel as the creator and governor of history, as the bestower of wisdom and righteous judge. It behooves men to strive for the true wisdom that reverences God fittingly. This is the purpose of life, since death severs man's relationship with God. Therefore, the righteous man may expect to receive his reward for good conduct, in this life (wisdom making good conduct possible), while punishment befalls the sinner and unbeliever.

Baruch

Text: Greek—Swete, III:351–59; Rahlfs, II:748–56; LXX Gott, XV:450–67. Latin—*Vulgata*, II:1255–65. Sahidic—*P. Bodmer XXII et Mississippi Coptic Codex II: Baruch 1:1–5:5 en sahidique*, Cologny-Genève, 1964. Fritzsche-Grimm (O. F. Fritzsche).

Translations: Charles (Whitehouse), I:569–95; Kautzsch (Rothstein), I:213–25; BOuT (B. Wambacq), 1967; Echter-B (V. Hamp), 1950; Herder-B (H. Schneider), 1954; Jerusalem-B (A. Gelin), 2nd ed., 1959; J. J. Crowley, *The Books of Lamentations, Baruch, Sophonia, Nahum and Habacuc with a Commentary*, Pamphlet Bible Series, 1962; C. Amantini and S. Orienti, "Baruch," *BSanct*, II (1962):897–900.

Monographs: B. N. Wambacq, "Les prières de Baruch (1:15–2:19) et de Daniel (9:5–19)," *Bibl*, XL (1959):463–75; *idem*, "L'unité littèraire de Baruch I–III 8," *BETL*, XII (1959):455–60; *idem*, "L'unité du livre de Baruch," *Bibl*, XXXVII (1966):574–76; A. Kniazef, "Baroúch (hē bíblos),"

JUDAISM OUTSIDE THE HEBREW CANON

ThreskEthEnk, III (1963):646–50; E. Haenchen, "Das Buch Baruch," in *Gott und Mensch*, 1965, pp. 299–324.
BHH, I:202–203 (M. Weise); *RGG*, I:900–903 (O. Plöger, W. Werbeck); Eissfeldt, pp. 802–5 (English: 592–94); *IDB*, I:362–63 (S. Tedesche).

Text

The book has been preserved in Greek in the majority of the majuscules (though not in Sinaiticus or Codex C) and in numerous minuscules. In three passages in the Hexapla, however, Origen states that a clause is not present in the Hebrew, which means that he still knew of a Hebrew original. Jerome did not and so did not discuss it. The earlier Syriac translation is based on the Greek translation and the Hebrew original; this is the Syriac version included by Walton in his Polyglot and by P. de Lagarde. There is also a second Syriac translation preserved in the Syrohexapla of Bishop Paul of Tella; it dates from the year 618. The Old Latin was translated from the Greek. There are also Coptic, Ethiopic, Armenian, and Arabic translations of the Greek text.

According to J. J. Kneucker, the lost original text contained the entire book. Other scholars today assume a Hebrew original only for the first two sections, 1:1–4:4. They base this conclusion on the Hebraic style of this part of the book, its numerous Hebraisms, retention of the terms *manna* and *minha* in 1:10, and several mistranslations. In the final section, 4:5–5:9, the Greek style is better. Such an expression as "ten times more" in 4:28 can hardly derive from a Hebrew original, so that despite the hebraizing parallelism, this section can hardly be assumed to have a Hebrew original.

Contents

Chapter 1:1-14 is an historical introduction, telling how Baruch wrote a letter in Babylon and read it aloud there. The exiles are now sending it to Jerusalem, together with a collection of money, so that it may be publicly read there on

70

feasts and other appropriate occasions and that sacrifices may be offered for the benefit of Nebuchadnezzar and his son Balthasar. 1:15–3:8 contains a penitential prayer in prose, which becomes a kind of sermon and concludes once more as a penitential prayer. 3:9–4:4 contains a metrical hymn in praise of wisdom: it is a gift of God to Israel, but has been ignored and must now be searched for as the most precious of treasures. 4:5–5:9 consists of seven short metrical units (4:5-9*a*, 9*b*-16, 17-29, 30-35; 4:36–5:4; 5:5-9). In 4:9*b*-16 and 4:17-29, the city of Jerusalem laments her distress; in the other passages the poet or God himself speaks comforting words of hope for approaching deliverance.

Historical Problems

The book purports to be the work of the prophet Jeremiah's companion and scribe, whose genealogy is traced back three generations beyond Jeremiah 32:12. The author is said to have been present in Babylon with those who were deported in 597 and, in particular, with Jeconiah, the king of Judah, when Nebuchadnezzar destroyed Jerusalem. This statement contradicts the book of Jeremiah. As in the book of Daniel, Nebuchadnezzar is said to have had a son Balthasar. In actuality the latter was a son of the last Babylonian king, Nabonidus. Some minor features, such as the return of the silver Temple vessels made by Hezekiah, are also historically improbable. Like the book of Daniel, therefore, the book pretends to have been composed at an early date by a contemporary of Jeremiah; in other words, like the book of Daniel, it is pseudepigraphic.

1:2 shows that Jerusalem has fallen into the hands of the enemy and been burned. This took place in 587 B.C., but not in 63 B.C. when Pompey took Jerusalem; it did take place, however, in A.D. 70 when Titus captured the city. But is the burning merely a reminiscence of 587 or a present reality? That is the question. If the reader takes his clue from the burning of the city, the names "Nebuchadnezzar" and "Balthasar" could stand for Vespasian and Titus; this seems more likely than Pompey and Caesar. This would mean that the final redaction of the book took place shortly after A.D. 70.

The various sections of Baruch, however, may well have been in existence prior to the final redaction and so must be investigated individually. The penitential prayer is closely related to Daniel 9. Either this prayer was the prototype for Daniel, or both Daniel 9 and Baruch 1:15–3:8 are both based on an earlier prayer that has been lost. It is therefore possible that this penitential prayer might date back to the oppression of Antiochus IV Epiphanes. No other concrete evidence permits a more precise dating. The hymn to wisdom exhibits several similarities to Proverbs 28, Job, and especially Sirach, so that for this hymn, the year 180 B.C. represents a *terminus post quem*. The poems of promise in 4:13ff. exhibit a kinship with Deutero-Isaiah; 4:36ff. is almost identical word-for-word with Psalm 11 of the Psalms of Solomon, which date from the middle of the first century B.C. We therefore conclude that the individual sections of the book may date from the second and first century B.C., but that the book as a whole was not put together and provided with its historical introduction until after A.D. 70.

Setting

The purpose of the book is clearly stated at the outset—that is, public reading during worship "on the occasion of festivals and on appropriate days." It is possible to understand the former expression as referring to the great festivals; more likely, however, it refers to the observance of the ninth of Ab in memory of the destruction of Jerusalem. "Appropriate days" probably refers to specially appointed days of mourning and fasting. *Apostolic constitutions* v. 20 in fact states that Baruch was read on the tenth of Gorpiaios during synagogue worship. It is also possible to interpret Ephraem Syrus *Opp. Syr.* iii. 212 as referring to this practice (E. Schürer, III:464).

Author

The author or authors apparently lived in the Babylonian Diaspora—there is a close relationship with the school of Yohanan ben Zakkai (R. H. Charles).

Significance

The second part of the book in particular is characterized by the late Jewish idea that the Law is the sum of all wisdom and that God's solicitude for Israel is demonstrated by his gift of the Law. There seems to be no belief in any afterlife, so that men hope all the more for an imminent change of fortune.

Letter of Jeremiah

Text: Greek—Swete, III:379–84; Rahlfs, II:766–70; LXX Gott, XV:494–504. Latin—*Vulgata*, II:1262–65. Syriac—A. Mingana, "A New Jeremiah Apocryphon," BJRL, XI (1927):329–42, 352–437. Sahidic—*P. Bodmer XXII et Mississippi Coptic Codex II: Epître de Jèr en sahidique*, Cologny-Genève, 1964.

Translations: Charles (Ball), I:596–611; Kautzsch (Rothstein), I:226–29.

Commentaries: *HS* (E. Kalt), VII:3/4, 1932, pp. 7–8, 23–29; BOuT (B. N. Wambacq), 1957.

Monographs: E. S. Artom, "L'origine, la data e gli scopi dell'Epistola di Geremia," *Annuario Studi Ebr.*, I (1935):49–74; J. M Grintz, "הספרות העברית כבתקופת פרס," *Sefer H. Albeck*, 1963, pp. 123–51.

BHH, II:814 (B. M. Metzger); *RGG*, III:584 (M. Weise); Eissfeldt, pp. 805–6, 1022 (English: 594–95, 772); *IDB*, II:822–23 (S. Tedesche).

Text

The Letter of Jeremiah in Greek is contained in most of the uncials (not Sinaiticus) and minuscules. Of the various translations, the Arabic has independent value for reconstruction of the text.

Pace W. Rothstein, who thinks the work was originally written in Greek, a Hebrew original should be assumed, since this is the only way to explain two Greek mistranslations in verse 30 (*nhg* translated "go" instead of "lament") and verse 70 (*šš* translated as "marble" instead of "linen"). This hypothesis is further supported by fragments of five or six manuscripts from Cave 4 at Qumran containing an apocryphon closely related to Baruch and the Letter of Jeremiah (M. Burrows); papyrus fragments containing the Greek text of the Letter have been discovered in Cave 7 (*RB*, LXIII (1956): 572).

Contents

The book is a satirical sermon against idolatry organized around the rhetorical question, "Who could say that such gods are gods?" which is repeated nine times. Prototypes may be found in Isaiah 44:9-20 and Jeremiah 10:1-6, except that here the satire is in prose rather than poetry.

Place and Date

The date and place of the book's origin are obscure. The Qumran evidence shows that the Greek translation was in existence at least by the first century C.E. If the phrase "to Babylon" is intended to be a veiled reference to Rome, the Hebrew text could be dated as late as the time of Pompey, that is, the middle of the first century B.C. It is possible, however, that "Babylon" is not a fiction. In this case, although the sixth century is probably impossible, the Persian period is conceivable, even though in that time period gold and silver idols could hardly have been a temptation. A later date is therefore more reasonable.

Significance

The Letter alludes to a danger threatening those to whom the sermon is addressed—assimilation to paganism. The tone of irony shows that this apostasy is due not to oppression but to a need for recognition. It is not so much stigmatized for being sinful as censured for being ridiculous.

I Maccabees

Text: Greek—Swete, III:594–661; Rahlfs, I:1039–99; LXX Gott, IX (W. Kappler). Latin—*Vulgata*, II:1432–80; Fritzsche-Grimm (W. Grimm).

Translations: Charles (W. O. E. Oesterley), I:59–124; Kautzsch (E. Kautzsch), I:24–81; Clamer-B (M. Grandclaudon), 1951; Echter-B (D. Schötz), 1948; Jerusalem-B (F. M. Abel and J. Starcky), 3rd ed., 1961; *JewApocrLit* (S. S. Tedesche, S. Zeitlin), 1950; Kahana, 2nd ed., 1956; *SaBi* (M. Laconi), 1960; S. Tedesche, *The Book of Maccabees*, 1962.

Commentaries: *HS* (H. Bévenot), 1931; J. C. Dancy, 1954; C. Gutberlet, 1920; E. Weinfeld, *Los Macabeos*, 1963.

Monographs: F. M. Abel, "Topographie des campagnes machabéennes," *RB*, XXXII (1923):495–521; XXXIII (1924):201–17, 371–87; XXXIV (1925):194–216; XXXV (1926):206–22, 510–33; H. W. Ettelson, *The Integrity of I Maccabees*, 1925; B. Niese, *Kritik der beiden Makkabäerbücher*, 1900; H. Willrich, *Urkundenfälschung in der hellenistisch-jüdischen Literatur*, FRLANT, 38, 1924; L. Rabinowitz, "The First Essenes," *JSSt*, IV (1959):338–61; F. Gryglewicz, "Le codex Alexandrinus du premier livre des Macchabées," RoczTKan, VIII (1961):23–37; R. Hanhart, *Zur Zeitrechnung des I. und II. Makkabäerbuches*, BZAW, 88, 1964; M. V. Arrabal and P. Bellet, "Macabeos," *EncBib*, IV (1965):1132–37; B. Loth and A. Michel, "Macchabées (Livres de)," *DTC*, Table gen. XII (1965):3047–51; M. Adinolfi, "Il testamento di Mattatia e i suoi esempi etigi (1 Mac 2:49-69)," *FrancLA*, XV (1964/65):74–97; A. Penna, "I Libri dei Maccabei nei manuscritti siriaci della Bibliotheca Vaticana," *Mél E. Tisserant*, I (1964):325–43; J. A. Palacios, "Siméon macabeo," *EncBib*, VI (1965):702 ff.; A. Penna, "*Diathḗkē* e *synthḗkē* nei libri dei Maccabei," *Bib*, XLVI (1965):149–80; I. V. Oikonomos, "*Makkabaîoi*," *Thresk-*

EthEnk, VIII (1966):507–11; E. Blumenthal and S. Morenz, "Spuren ägyptischer Königsideologie in einem Hymnus auf den Makkabäerfürsten Simon," *ZÄS,* XCIII (1966):21–29; R. Hanhart, "Kriterien geschichtlicher Wahrheit in der Makkabäerzeit," Fourth World Congress of Jewish Studies, Papers, I (1967):81–85.

BHH, II:1126–30 (R. Hanhart); *RGG,* IV:620–21 (K.-D. Schunck); Eissfeldt, pp. 781–85, 1021 (English: 576–79, 771); *IDB,* III:203–6 (W. H. Brownlee).

Text

The text of I Maccabees is preserved in Greek in the three uncials Sinaiticus, A, and V, as well as in several minuscules. Of these minuscules, 52, 56, 62, 107, and 107*a* agree for the most part with the uncials, while 19, 64, and 93*d* contain the Lucianic recension, which, however, diverges less from other manuscripts here than elsewhere. The Syriac Peshitta derives from this Lucianic recension, while the Latin Codex Ambrosianus follows the uncials. The Old Latin version comprises two recensions—one in the Codex Sangermanensis, the other a smoother translation borrowed by the Vulgate.

The book was originally composed in Hebrew. Origen records the title as *Sarbēth Sabanaiel,* שר בית שבני אל ("Leader of the House of the Sons of God" [?]). Jerome writes in the *Prologus galeatus,* "Machabaeorum primum librum hebraicum reperi." Hebraisms in the Greek text mark it as a translation from Hebrew rather than Aramaic.

Contents

After a short account of Alexander the Great (1:1-9), the actual narrative begins with the accession to power of Antiochus IV Epiphanes (175–164 B.C.) and recounts the measures he took to suppress the Jewish religion (1:10-64). The resistance to his attack on orthodox Judaism, encouraged by Mattathias, a priest from Modein, is recorded in 2:1-70. The battles, victories and death of Judas Maccabeus constitute the subject matter of 3:1–9:22. The seesaw battles and political changes under Jonathan are described in 9:23–12:53. The deeds of Simon, the last of the sons of Mattathias, are set forth in 13:1–16:24. A forty-year period of kaleidoscopic events—from the accession of Antiochus IV Epiphanes (175 B.C.) to the death of Simon (135 B.C.)—is depicted in a simple but impressive style.

Unity

The book poses two problems. The first derives from the fact that although Josephus for the most part follows the historical narrative of I Maccabees, he seems not to know chapters 14–16. The question is whether he never saw these concluding chapters or chose not to use their account. They probably constituted a part of I Maccabees from the very beginning, since there is no stylistic or thematic break from it. The situation is different in the case of 14:16ff., where the letter from Sparta has apparently been interpolated somewhat awkwardly into a report about relations with Rome. Possibly the letter from Sparta was noted in te margin, whence it later made its way into the text without being completely assimilated.

Historical Problems

The relationship between I and II Maccabees will be discussed in the section devoted to the latter. Here we shall discuss the interspersed letters, whose function in making the historical narrative vivid and convincing must not be ignored. These are: (1) the letter of the Jews in Gilead to Jonathan and his brothers (5:10-13); (2) the decree making the office of high priest hereditary within the Hasmonean family (14:27-45); (3) a letter from the Roman senate to the Jewish nation (8:23-32); (4) a letter from the Romans to the kings and their lands (15:16-21); (5) a letter from Jonathan to the Spartans (12:6-18); (6) a letter from the king of Sparta to the high priest Onias I (12:20-23); (7) a letter from the Spartans to Simon (14:20-23); (8) a letter from Demetrius I to Jonathan (10:3-6); (9) from Alexander Balas to Jonathan (10:18-20); (10) from Demetrius I to

Jonathan (10:25-45); (11) from Demetrius II to Jonathan (11:29-37); (12) from Demetrius II to Simon (13:36-40); and (13) from Antiochus VII Sidetes to Simon (15:1-9).

The first letter comprises only a short and probably stylized summary of its contents; it lacks the usual preface mentioning sender and recipient and containing formulas of greeting. It was certainly originally composed in Hebrew. Whether it was incorporated into the Hebrew original of I Maccabees in its present abbreviated and edited form or was not altered until the book was translated into Greek cannot be determined with certainty.

Linguistically, letter number two would represent the same situation if it was originally composed in Hebrew, as we may assume. When it was translated into Greek, it may well have been revised and embellished in ways that we can no longer determine since we do not have the original decree.

All the other letters were first translated into Hebrew and then later retranslated into Greek by the translator of I Maccabees, probably without reference to the originals (if indeed the originals were still extant). Since their language is identical with that of their textual environment, it is hardly to be hoped that their official tenor was preserved when they were retranslated; it is more likely that the principle of stylistic unity controlled the translation. It is obvious that proofs of political favor could have been added in the process and, as is quite possible, that the contents of the letters were merely summarized. We may therefore conclude that the skepticism of scholars like U. Willrich as to the genuineness of these documents is hardly justified; letters of this sort were in fact written. This does not mean, however, that we can say anything certain about the wording of individual letters or the genuineness of others.

Genre

I Maccabees is an historical narrative depicting clearly and vividly forty years in the life of the Jews clustered

78

about Jerusalem, a period filled with momentous events, intrigues of all kinds, defeats, and victories. Interpolated documents, speeches (2:49-68; 3:18-22; 4:8-11; 13:3-6; 16:2-3), prayers (4:30-33), laments (2:7-13; 3:50-58), and psalms of victory (4:24) enliven the narrative, but there are no exaggerated claims of miraculous intervention by heavenly powers. Men contest with other men under the governance of God. Thus I Maccabees stands in the best tradition of Israelite historiography as exemplified by the court history of David and, for the most part, by the books of Kings and Ezra.

Author

The author was probably a Jew living in Jerusalem and was a supporter of the Maccabean party not only because of its esteem for the Law and customs of the fathers, but also because of its sense of realism (defense on the sabbath!). Though neither a Pharisee nor a Sadducee, he was more nearly the latter than anything else. He may have been a member of the family of the Maccabees and written the story of his ancestors for this reason, but this is only a possibility. He seems at least to have had access to archives, which suggests that he held an important position.

Date

The book concludes with a formula modeled after the concluding formulas of the books of Kings, which appears to presuppose the death of John Hyrcanus (134–103). The year 103 is therefore the earliest the book can be dated. The friendly attitude it displays toward the Romans makes it unlikely that relationships with Rome had already been clouded by the arrival of Pompey in 63 B.C. The book should therefore be dated between 103 and 63 B.C.; the same period probably also witnessed its translation into Greek.

Significance

I Maccabees shows us a Judaism in which the ruling classes are prepared for political reasons to cooperate with

Antiochus IV Epiphanes in his efforts to establish uniformity, while a simple country priest holding fast to the Law and to ancestral custom summons the people to resist, delivers them, and finally sees the fruition of his work in his sons. Faithful obedience to the Law, properly interpreted (mortal danger obviates observance of the sabbath), is crowned with success by God.

II Maccabees

Text: Greek—Swete, III:662–708; Rahlfs, I:1099–1139; LXX Gott, IX/2 (W. Kappler, R. Hanhart), 1959. Latin—*Vulgata*, II:1480–1512. Fritzsche-Grimm (W. Grimm).

Translations: Charles (J. Moffat), I:125–154; Kautzsch (A. H. H. Kamphausen), I:81–119; Clamer-B (M. Grandclaudon), 1951; EB (F.-M. Abel), 1949; Echter-B (D. Schötz), 1948; Jerusalem-B (F.-M. Abel and J. Starcky), 3rd ed., 1961; *JewApocrLit* (S. S. Tedesche and S. Zeitlin), 1954; *SaBi* (M. Laconi), 1960.

Commentaries: *HS* (H. Bévenot), 1931; C. Gutberlet, 1927; J. Obersi, *II Knjiga Makabejska*, 1965.

Monographs: E. Bickermann, "Ein jüdischer Festbrief vom Jahre 124 v. Chr. (II Macc 1:1-19)," *ZNW*, XXXII (1933):233–54; P. Katz, "The Text of 2 Maccabees Reconsidered," *ZNW*, LI (1960):10–30; R. Laqueur, *Kritische Untersuchungen zum zweiten Makkabäerbuch*, 1906; C. C. Torrey, "The Letters Prefixed to Second Maccabees," *JAOS*, LX (1940):119–50; W. H. Willis, "The New Collections of Papyri at the University of Mississippi," *Proceedings of the IX International Congress of Papyrology*, Oslo, 1958 (1961), pp. 381–92, pls. V–VI; R. Hanhart, "Zum Text des 2. u. 3. Makkabäerbuches," *NAWG*, Phil.-hist. Klasse, 1961, pp. 427–86.

BHH, II:1126–30 (R. Hanhart); *RGG*, IV:621–22 (K.-D. Schunck and W. Werbeck); Eissfeldt, pp. 785–88 (English: 579–81, 771); *IDB*, III:206–10 (W. H. Brownlee).

Text

While the two letters preserved in 1:1–2:18—if
genuine—were probably originally composed in Hebrew,
2:19–15:40 was undoubtedly framed in Greek from the
very outset. Today the entire book is extant only in Greek.
The only uncial with a complete text is A; V contains a
fragmentary text. There are also a number of minuscules.
Alongside these, the Old Latin translation is also a valuable
witness; Jerome included it without change in the Vulgate.
A different Latin translation is found in Codex Ambrosianus and Codex Complutensis. The Syriac translation
is a paraphrase and is of little value for textual criticism.

Contents

The book is divided into two sections. The first
comprises two letters; the second and larger one purports
to be an epitome of the five books of the history of the
Maccabees written in Greek by Jason of Cyrene.

The first letter (1:1-10a) is from the Jerusalem Jews and
is addressed to the Jews in Egypt, telling them to celebrate
the Feast of Booths in Kislev of the year 143/142[?]. The
second letter is from the same group (1:10b–2:18); it is sent
to Aristobulus, the Jewish teacher of King Ptolemy VI
Philometor (181–146) or to his co-regent Ptolemy VII
Physkon (146–117) and the Jews of Egypt, exhorting them
through legends and miracle stories to join in celebrating
the Temple festival.

The second section of the book (2:19–15:40) begins with
a prologue (2:19-32). Next comes an historical narrative
(3:1–4:6) describing events under Seleucus IV (187–175).
The Hellenistic propaganda under Antiochus IV
Epiphanes (175–164) (4:7–5:27) and the persecution
beginning under him (6:1–7:42)—events such as the
murder of a mother and her seven sons—follow. Against
this dark background, 8:1-36 describes the successful
rebellion under Judas Maccabeus. The death of Antiochus
IV Epiphanes and the purification of the Temple are

described in 9:1–10:8, battles with neighbors in 10:9-38, and the first campaign of the regent Lysias and the conclusion of peace in 11:1-38. Further battles with neighboring cities and peoples are recorded in 12:1-45; the second campaign of Lysias is reported in 13:1-26; and the campaign of Nicanor (162 B.C.), in 14:1–15:37. A personal note concludes the book (15:38-40).

Jason of Cyrene and the Epitomator

According to 2:23, Jason of Cyrene wrote five books in Greek recounting the events leading up to the Maccabean revolt and the history of the Maccabees or of Judas Maccabeus. 3:1–15:37 purports to be a summary taken from this history. Nothing else is known of the author or of his work in five books. If the style of the author of II Maccabees gives us a clue to that of Jason, he was a practitioner of the elevated historiography typical of contemporary Hellenism, whose intention was less to record the precise course of events than to achieve a rhetorical effect through the concatenation of episodes. Thus Jason of Cyrene (in North Africa) was a Jewish historian open to Hellenistic culture and trained in rhetoric, who adhered to the Law despite his Hellenistic education. He probably composed his work around the year 100 B.C.

The anonymous epitomator, the author of II Maccabees, by his own statement omitted details and numbers from his work and strove to produce a brief summary. Were the concluding formulas in 3:40; 7:42; 10:8; 13:26 and 15:38ff. that mark off the individual sections identical with the conclusions of each of Jason's books, we could say more about the way the epitomator worked. The miracle stories he ascribes to Jason. But whether Jason also exhibited the anti-Hasmonean attitude that comes to light in 10:1 and 15:1ff., as well as the pro-Pharisaic bias evident in the emphasis on both the resurrection of the dead (7:14, 23, 29, 36) and the scribal office of Eleazar (6:18ff.), is dubious. Here we may see the characteristic hand of the epitomator. The epitomator wrote his book very shortly after Jason's work appeared.

The Letters

The epitomator prefixed two letters (1:1-10*a* and 1:10*b*–2:18) to his summary of Jason. There are also a letter of Antiochus IV Epiphanes (9:19-27), one of Lysias (11:16-21), two from Antiochus V Eupator (164 B.C.) (16:22-26 and 16:27-33), and one letter from the Romans (16:34-38).

With regard to the first two letters, one could assume a considerably revised Hebrew original for the first and possibly for the second, as well. In the latter case, however, the original would have been so distorted by interpolations and expansions that it appears more appropriate to consider this letter a fictitious epistle. For the other letters, there is a possibility that similar documents were extant but were considerably edited by the author [Jason? the epitomator?] and assimilated to the style of the book as a whole.

Historical Problems

The book raises two historical problems. Contrary to the actual facts and to the account in I Maccabees, Antiochus IV Epiphanes dies before the purification of the Temple, and Judas Maccabeus defeats Lysias after the dedication of the Temple. There are various explanations of the discrepancy. Eissfeldt attributes it to the fact that the two letters prefixed by the epitomator presuppose the death of Antiochus and call on their recipients to celebrate the dedication of the Temple. Others suggest that either Jason or the epitomator wanted to tell the story of Antiochus to its end before discussing the dedication of the Temple, and that he wanted to bracket the two campaigns of Lysias. In any case, II Maccabees here takes considerable liberties with the actual course of history.

JUDAISM OUTSIDE THE HEBREW CANON

Significance

In its theological doctrines, II Maccabees exhibits several advances beyond the Old Testament and thus exhibits important points of contact with the New Testament. Here we find the first explicit statement of creation *ex nihilo* (7:28). The book espouses the resurrection of the dead, at least of the righteous (7:9, 14, 23, 29).

Additions to Esther

Text: Greek—Swete, II:755–56, 762–63, 765–66, 767–68, 773–75, 779–80; Rahlfs, I:951–52, 957–58, 960–61, 962, 967–69, 973; LXX Gott, VIII/3:131–35, 153–56, 161–71, 189–95, 206–207. Latin—*Vulgata*, I:724–30; *Biblia Sacra*, IX:15–66. Fritzsche-Grimm (O. F. Fritzsche).

Translations: Charles (J. A. F. Gregg), I:665–84; Kautzsch (V. Ryssel), I:193–212; Echter-B (F. Stummer), 1950; Herder-B (H. Bückers), 1953; Jerusalem-B (A. Barucq), 1952; Kahana (M. Stein), 2nd ed., 1956.

Commentaries: J. B. Schildenberger (*HS*), 1941; S. Grzybek; S. Baksik; S. Grzybek, *Ksiegi Tobiasza, Judyty, Estery*, Wstep-Przeklad z Oryginalu-Komentarz, 6:1-3, 1963.

Monographs: D. Abrudan, "Sarbatorile postexilice ale Evreilor," *Studi Teol* (Bucharest), XIV (1963):489–501; B. Girbau, "Ester," *EncBib*, III (1964):229–32; S. H. Horn, "Mordecai, a Historical Problem," *BiRes*, IX (1964):14–25; A. Kniazef, "Esthēr," *ThreskEthEnk*, V (1964):905–8; H. Rogovin, "Was the Book of Esther Read During the Second Temple?" *Bitzaron*, XLVII (1964):177–79; *idem*, "תקופת מגילת אסתר באספקלריה של יוסף בן מתתיהו," *Bitzaron*, LI (1965):146–50; C. Schedl, "Das Buch Esther, Roman oder Geschichte?" *TGegw*, VII (1964):85–93; R. M. Seyberlich, "Esther in der Septuaginta und bei Flavius Josephus," in *Neue Beiträge zur Geschichte der Alten Welt*, ed. E. C. Welskopf (1964): pp. 363–66; A. Kerib, "מגלה של גלות," *כרמלית*, IX (1963):10–27; G. J. Botterweck, "Die Gattung des Buches Esther im Spektrum neuerer Publikationen," *BiLeb*, V

(1964):274–92; W. H. Brownlee, "Le livre grec d'Esther et la royauté divine," *RB*, LXXIII (1966):161–85; Aser Weiser, "מגילת אסתר," *Sefer Y. F. Korngrün*, 1964; R. Weiss, "מחניים "לשונה וסגנונה של מגילת אסתר", CIV (1966).

BHH, I:445–46 (H. Ringgren); *RGG*, II:708 (M. Weise); Eissfeldt, pp. 800–802 (English: 591–92); *IDB*, II:151–53 (V. R. Gold).

Text

The Additions to Esther are integral components of the Greek version of the Book of Esther and thus share in the history of the Greek text of this book. Thus the unrevised text of the third century is found in the majuscules B, A, Sinaiticus, and N, and the minuscules 55, 108, and 249; the recension of Origen is found in 93 and 93*b;* that of Hesychius, in 44, 68, 71, 76, 106, 107, 120, and 236; and that of Lucian, in 19, 93*a,* and 108*b.* The last of these has tightened up the text by omitting 12:1-6; 9:1-2, 5-19; and 11:1. The Old Latin follows this recension. Jerome placed the Additions at the end of the book with the comment that he did not find them in the Hebrew. Two targums preserve the Book of Esther with even further additions; it was very popular among the Jews in the early Middle Ages and was recounted with extensive elaborations. There is no Syriac text of the Additions. They are preserved, however, in Coptic, Ethiopic, and Armenian. The Book of Esther has not been found at Qumran.

Contents

We are dealing with six additions in ten sections: (1) the dream of Mordecai (Swete, A, 1–11; Rahlfs, 1, 1*a-l;* Vulgate, 11:2-12; Luther, 7:1-9); (2) the conspiracy against Artaxerxes (Swete, A, 12–17; Rahlfs, 1, l*m-r;* Vulgate, 12:16; not in Luther); (3) edict on extermination of the Jews (Swete, B, 1-7; Rahlfs, 3, 13*a-g;* Vulgate, 13:1-7; Luther, 1:1-4); (4) prayer of Mordecai (Swete, C, 1-11; Rahlfs, 4, 17*a-i;* Vulgate, 13:8-18; Luther, 2:1-8); (5) prayer of Esther (Swete, C, 12-30; Rahlfs, 4, 17*k-z;* Vulgate,

14:1-19; Luther, 3:1-12); (6) Esther before Artaxerxes (Swete, D, 1-16; Rahlfs, 5, *la-2b;* Vulgate, 15:4-19; Luther, 4:3-14); (7) edict in favor of the Jews (Swete, E, 1–24; Rahlfs, 8, *12a-x;* Vulgate, 16:1-24; Luther, 6:1-16); (8) interpretation of the initial dream (Swete, F, 1–10; Rahlfs, 10, *3a-k;* Vulgate, 10:4-13; Luther, 9:1-7); and (9) naming of the translator (Swete, F, 11; Rahlfs, 10, *3l;* Vulgate, 11:1; Luther, 5:1).

The points at which these passages occur in the canonical Book of Esther are indicated in the citations from Rahlfs. Apart from the dream and its interpretation, we are dealing with two related decrees of Artaxerxes and with two penitential prayers, one of Mordecai and one of Esther, recorded in detail, together with an elaboration of Esther's appearance before Artaxerxes.

Original Text

While earlier Catholic scholarship considered the possibility of translation from Hebrew or Aramaic, it has more recently accepted the view of non-Catholic scholarship, which holds that the Additions were originally composed in Greek. Ryssel had already pointed out that the Greek of the decrees is significantly better than that of the other Additions, which are composed in a Greek similar to that of the Septuagint. Eissfeldt considers it possible that only the two decrees were in Greek from the very outset, while the other Additions were translated from the Hebrew. The point must be conceded. The decrees may have used official documents from the Ptolemaic or Seleucid chancery as stylistic prototypes. The other sections may derive from Hebrew oral tradition.

Author and Date

The conclusion of the Greek Book of Esther states that a certain Dositheos (supposedly a Levitical priest) and Ptolemaeus brought a Purim letter in the fourth year of the reign of Ptolemy and Cleopatra; they asserted its authenticity and said that it had been translated by Lysimachus, the son of Ptolemaeus, who belonged to those who lived in Jerusalem. If this account is trustworthy, we can only be dealing with Ptolemy VIII (117/6–108/7) or Ptolemy XII (Eissfeldt's suggestion), in other words, the year 114 or 78/77. But the emphasis on translation might mean that what is referred to is the book minus the Additions, in other words, translation of the Hebrew text. Then the Additions would date toward the end of the first century B.C. F. Altheim and R. Stiehl, on the contrary, prefer a date around 130 B.C., the period before the rise of the Arsacid Mithridates. This dating would best explain why, contrary to the canonical book, Haman is branded a Macedonian, thus being denounced as an alien.

The author of the Additions was a Jew who probably lived in Jerusalem as part of a colony of Diaspora Jews from Egypt.

Significance

The Additions to Esther serve to satisfy the curiosity of the reader about certain questions and also to enhance the edifying nature of the book.

Additions to Daniel

(a) Susanna
(b) Prayer of Azariah and Song of the Three Young Men
(c) Bel and the Dragon

Text: Greek—Swete, III:576–93, 518–23; Rahlfs, II:864–70, 885–94, 936–41; LXX Gott, XVI:80–91, 120–32, 213–23. Latin—*Vulgata,* II:1368–73, 1348–51; Fritzsche-Grimm (O. F. Fritzsche).

Translations: Charles (W. H. Bennett, D. M. Kay, and T. W. Davies), I:625–64; Kautzsch (J. W. Rothstein), I:172–93; *BOuT* (J. T. Nelis), 1954; Kahana (B. Heller), 2nd ed., 1956.

Commentaries: A. Scholz, *Commentar über das Buch Esther*

mit seinen Zusätzen und über Susanna, 1892; *idem, Commentar über das Buch Judith und über Bel und Drache,* 2nd ed., 1896; G. Rinaldi, *Daniele,* La S. Bibbia, 1962.

Monographs: C. W. Baumgartner, "Susanna; die Geschichte einer Legende," *ARW,* XXIV (1926):259–80, reprinted in his *Gesammelte Aufsätze zum Alten Testament,* 1959, pp. 42–66; *idem,* "Der weise Knabe und die des Ehebruchs beschuldigte Frau," *ARW,* XXVII (1929):187–88, reprinted in his *Gesammelte Aufsätze zum Alten Testament,* 1959, pp. 66–67; M. Wurmbrand, *A Falasha Variant of the Story of Susanna,* 1963; J. M. Grintz, "הספרות העברית כבתקופת פרס," in *Sefer H. Albeck,* 1963, pp. 123–51.

(b) C. Kuhl, *Die drei Männer im Feuer,* 1930.
(c) F. Zimmermann, "Bel and the Dragon," *VT,* VIII (1958):438–40.

BHH, I:318–20 (F. Michaeli); *ibid.,* "Asarja, Gebet des," I:135 (F. Michaeli); *ibid.,* "Bel zu Babel," I:214 (M. A. Beek); *ibid.,* "Drache zu Babel," I:354 (F. Michaeli); *ibid.,* "Susanna," III, 1896 (E. Kamlah); *RGG,* II:2631 (W. Baumgartner; W. Werbeck); *ibid.,* "Asarjagebet," I:637 (M. Weise); *ibid.,* "Bel zu Babel," I:1017 (M. Weise); *ibid.,* "Drache zu Babel," II:260 (M. Weise); *ibid.,* "Susannabuch," VI:532 (M. Weise); Eissfeldt, pp. 797–800 (English: 588–90).

In the Greek Bible, the book of Daniel includes three additions not found in the Hebrew Canon: (a) Susanna; (b) the Song of the Three Young Men; and (c) Bel and the Dragon.

Text

The textual tradition of the Additions is the same as that of the canonical books—the Septuagint and Theodotion. The Septuagint text is preserved only in Codex 88 (Chisianus), the Syrohexapla, and (fragmentarily) in Papyrus 967. The uncials and minuscules give the Theodotion text, since it had very early supplanted the Septuagint. While the Syrohexapla furnishes the Septuagint text of Origen, the Syriac translation as found in Walton's polyglot and P. A. de Lagarde is based on the text of Theodotion. Theodotion is also the textual basis for the Old Latin, Coptic, Ethiopic, Arabic, and Armenian translations. The extent to which the Additions may be based on original texts in Hebrew or Aramaic cannot be determined with certainty. Each of the three Additions raises its own special problems, which will be examined in the following discussion.

(a) Susanna

Traditio-Historical Problems

The Septuagint and Theodotion diverge widely in their narrative content; linguistically, however, they are so alike as to be identical word for word in certain passages. Two explanations have been offered for this linguistic assimilation. Theodotion may have had the Septuagint before him or in his memory when writing his story of Susanna, or an assimilation may have taken place later, albeit very early. It is hard to decide between the two possibilities, although it seems most likely that memory played a part. In any event Theodotion furnishes the more coherent narrative.

The story of Susanna is based on two motifs—the wife accused falsely and the judgment of the youth whose wisdom surpasses that of the elder judges. In the earliest stratum the young judge is anonymous. But as early as the Septuagint, the name of Daniel is interpolated, which turns the narrative into a story of the youth of that famous man. In Theodotion the scene is set in Babylon and the judgment given by Daniel is set in bolder relief.

Contents

Susanna, the daughter of Hilkiah and wife of Joakim, arouses through her voluptuous beauty the lust of two elders, whose designs she repulses. They thereupon falsely accuse her of adultery, and she is condemned to death. Inspired by an angel, a young man named Daniel protests, takes separate depositions from the two accusers, convicts them of perjury, and puts them to death by having them thrown from a precipice and struck by a divine thunderbolt.

Genre

We are dealing with an edifying tale meant to make a point; an historical incident is possible but not demonstrable.

Author

The author was a Jew and probably lived in Palestine, since that is the only place where a death sentence could have been carried out. If the purpose of the narrative is to support the need for a more careful examination of witnesses, D. M. Kay has suggested the period of Simon ben Shetach, whose son was condemned to death on false evidence. Viewed in this light the Septuagint narrative could have come into being in the first half of the first century B.C.

Significance

The narrative demonstrates the superiority of the method espoused by the young, which requires separate examination of the two witnesses, to that of their elders, which considers the agreement of two witnesses sufficient.

In the final analysis, therefore, polemic intent was responsible for the preservation of the story; Daniel is the wise man supporting the new method.

(b) Prayer of Azariah
and Song of the Three Young Men

Text

Everything said above about the textual tradition of the Additions to Daniel applies, with the difference that here the Septuagint and Theodotion do not exhibit many differences. A Hebrew original is likely.

Contents and Structure

Both the Septuagint and Theodotion insert the Additions after 3:23 of the Masoretic text. A brief prose introduction (3:24-25) is followed by the Prayer of Azariah (3:26-45); another short bridge section in prose (3:46-51) is followed by the Song of the Three Young Men (3:52-90). The Prayer of Azariah is a communal lament in the first person plural. It begins with an exhomologesis praising God's greatness and righteousness and continues with a confession of sins and a description of distress. The bridge section describes the heating of the furnace, whose flames finally consume the men who are tending it, while an angel joins the three young men and turns the heat inside the oven into a refreshing breeze. The Song of the Three Young Men is a hymn in litany form praising God's omnipotence; in form it resembles Psalm 136, in content, Psalm 148.

Place and Date

The three sections of the interpolation came into being separately. The second section might originally have been part of the Masoretic text of the book of Daniel and therefore could have been written in Aramaic. This hypothesis would mean that the first and third sections of the interpolation were inserted into the Masoretic text and then later removed from it together with the bridge section. There is no compelling evidence that this explanation accounts for the discontinuity in the Masoretic text, but it is a possibility.

Verse 38 of the penitential prayer indicates that there is no king, no prophet, no leader, no burnt offering, no sacrifice, no incense. This statement could refer to the period of Antiochus IV Epiphanes (175–164); the period after A.D. 70 would be too late, the Exile too early. This would naturally suggest Palestine as a place of origin. In any case, the psalm is so inappropriate to the situation that it must have been occasioned by different circumstances and then found secondary application here. The same holds true for the third section, the hymn, which mentions the three men only in verse 88, with a reference to the setting as a reason for praising God. This passage, however, interrupts the regular structure and is therefore a secondary interpolation. Thus we are left with the impression that this hymn, too, is a secondary addition. Its place and date of origin cannot be determined.

Significance

The interpolation illustrates Psalm 50:15: If you call upon me in time of trouble, I will come to your rescue, and you will praise me.

(c) Bel and the Dragon

Text

See the general discussion of the Additions to Daniel. In Bel and the Dragon, the Septuagint differs markedly from Theodotion. Here, too, Theodotion tightens up the narrative by concentrating on the question of the living God. It is likely that the Septuagint had a Hebrew original. Whether Theodotion was familiar with the Hebrew or took the Septuagint as his point of departure is debatable; the latter seems the more likely alternative, since the two forms of the Greek text occasionally agree word for word.

Superscription

In the Septuagint, the narrative bears the superscription "From the prophecy of Habakkuk, son of Jesus, of the tribe of Levi;" it appears, therefore, at some time to have been appended to Habakkuk. But the appearance of Habakkuk constitutes only an episode in the narrative, which elsewhere has Daniel as its hero.

Contents

The title "Bel and the Dragon" covers two narratives that deal with the question of God: one focuses on the god Bel, or rather his statue in the temple of Bel in Babylon; the other has as its subject a serpent or dragon associated with this god, to which worship is offered. The king of Babylon (Cyrus, according to Theodotion), asks Daniel (the son of Habal, according to the Septuagint) why he does not worship Bel, for whom enormous quantities of food are prepared every day. A wager is arranged. Not the priests but the king himself has the food brought into the temple of Bel. He then seals the chamber of the god. According to Theodotion, Daniel, unbeknownst to the priests, strews ashes over the floor. During the night, the priests, together with their wives and children, enter the temple through a secret door. According to the Septuagint, they bring the food home with them; Theodotion apparently has them feast on it in the temple. The next morning, when the king has the seals opened, he is satisfied to observe that the food has vanished. Daniel, however, points out the footprints to him. When the king sees how the priests have deceived him, he has them slain and the temple of Bel destroyed.

The king does not yet admit defeat, however. He demands that Daniel admit that the serpent is indeed alive. Daniel asks the king to allow him to slay the serpent without using any weapon and makes cakes out of pitch, fat, and hair, which he tosses into the mouth of the serpent. The serpent bursts. The people demand that Daniel be put to death in the lion pit. Having been thrown to the lions, Daniel lives in the pit for seven days with seven lions; he is miraculously fed by Habakkuk. When seven days have passed, the king is overjoyed to see that Daniel is still alive and gives glory to the God of Daniel as the only God.

Author, Place, and Date

The narrative was composed by a Jew in order to demonstrate through examples that surpass the stories of the Masoretic Daniel that Yahweh is the only living God.

Since he knows even less of the real course of history than does the narrator of the Masoretic book of Daniel, he can hardly have lived before the Maccabean period. His work may be dated as late as the second half of the first century; if so, his polemic would be directed against the apostasy of worshiping Roman gods. An even later origin is possible; but, since Daniel is depicted as a table companion of the king rather than as a prisoner, the destruction of Jerusalem by Titus probably represents the latest possible date.

Significance

In his two narratives the author shows that pagan deities are worshiped because their priests deceive the people; they are not truly alive. According to Theodotion, the central question is the identity of the living God. The demonstration, however, does not go beyond rationalism.

Prayer of Manasseh

Text: Greek—Swete, III:824–26; Rahlfs, II:180–81; LXX Gott, X:361–63. Latin—*Vulgata,* II:1909. Syriac—H. Achelis and J. Flemming, *Die syrische Didaskalia,* 1904. Fritzsche-Grimm (O. F. Fritzsche).

Translations: Charles (H. E. Ryle), I:612–24; Kautzsch (V. Ryssel), I:165–71; Riessler, pp. 348–49, 1291; Kahana (E. S. Artom), 2nd ed., 1956.

Monographs: H. Volz, "Zur Überlieferung des Gebetes Manasses," *ZKG,* LXX (1959):293–307.

BHH, II:1137–38 (C. Westermann); *RGG,* IV:708 (W. Baumgartner); Eissfeldt, pp. 796–97 (English: 588, 771); *IDB,* III:255–56 (A. Wikgren).

Text

The earliest witness to the Prayer of Manasseh is the Didascalia, a work written in Greek but preserved only in a Syriac translation dating from the end of the second or the beginning of the third century. Here it is introduced by a passage reminiscent of II Chronicles 23:11-14. Together with the Didascalia, the Prayer of Manasseh was incorporated into the Constitutiones Apostolicae, which date from the fourth or fifth century. In Septuagint manuscripts it appears since the fifth century among the odes appended to the Psalms—that is, among the works meant for liturgical use. Among these odes it occupies the eighth or twelfth position. It was not included by the Vetus Latina or by Jerome. A translation made after Jerome is included by the Vulgate as an appendix. There are also Syriac, Armenian, Old Church Slavonic, and Arabic translations.

Contents

O. F. Fritzsche organizes the thirty-seven stichs of the Greek translation into fifteen verses as follows: 1-7, invocation and aretology; 8-12, confession of sins; 13, petition for forgiveness; and 14-15, thanksgiving.

Author, Date, and Place

That the prayer is of Jewish origin is indisputable. It can hardly have been composed in Hebrew, but its Jewish author probably wrote it in a Greek which contained echoes of Hebrew, in imitation of the structure of the penitential Psalms. It may have been written in Egypt. Since it was incorporated in a Christian book close to the end of the second century C.E., it must have been composed before then, perhaps as early as the second or first century B.C.

Significance

Contrary to the evidence of the books of Kings, Chronicles explains that the godless Manasseh ruled so long (fifty-five years) because he underwent a conversion during temporary captivity in Babylon. At some point in the development of this edifying theory of Chronicles (and in a form of the tradition no longer extant), this penitential psalm was composed as evidence of Manasseh's conversion and as an example of true repentance.

III Ezra

Text: Greek—Swete, II:129–61; Rahlfs, I:878–908. Latin—*Vulgata*, II:1910–30. Fritzsche-Grimm (O. F. Fritzsche).
Translations: Charles (S. A. Cook), I:1–58; Kautzsch (H. Guthe), I:1–23; Riessler, pp. 247–54, 1281–82; Kahana (A. Kahana), 2nd ed., 1956.
Commentaries: W. Rudolph (HAT, I/20), 1949.
Monographs: T. Denter, "Die Stellung der Bücher Esdras im Kanon des AT," dissertation, Fribourg, 1962, 1963; F. Zimmermann, "The Story of the Three Guardsmen," *JQR*, LIV (1963/64):179–200.
BHH, I:442–43 (L. H. Silberman); *RGG*, II:697 (W. Baumgartner); Eissfeldt, pp. 777–81, 1021 (English: 574–76, 771); *IDB*, II:140–42 (N. Turner).

Text

What the Vulgate calls "III Ezra" is preserved as "I Esdras" in the Greek Bible, where it appears in the majuscules B and A and in many minuscules. The book appears in Latin in the Vulgate manuscripts—A (Amiens, ninth century), Q (Paris, twelfth century), and Ω (Paris). Editions of the Septuagint place the book immediately before I Esdras, the Ezra and Nehemiah of the Hebrew Canon; in the Vulgate it follows the Prayer of Manasseh as a second supplement. Luther did not include it among the Apocrypha.

Title

The Greek Bible titles the book "I Esdras;" Alexandrinus adds "the priest." The Vulgate terms it "III Ezra."

Contents

The book may be incomplete not only at its conclusion, which comes in the middle of a sentence, but at its beginning (where the first words are, "And Josiah"). It comprises an independent translation of II Chronicles

35:1–36:23; Ezra 1:1-11; 2:1-3–3:13; 4:1–10:44; and Nehemiah 7:73–8:12 in a different sequence, with minor additions and omissions. In 3:1–5:6 the story of the three guardsmen, which is of Persian or perhaps East Semitic origin, is interpolated. The historical narrative recounts the Passover of Josiah, his death, the story of his successors and the destruction of Jerusalem, the Jews' deportation, and Cyrus' edict permitting the Jews to return and rebuild the Temple. It tells how the rebuilding was interrupted because the governor in Samaria objected, how more Jews returned under Darius and Zerubbabel, how the Temple was rebuilt under Zerubbabel and Joshua, how the Samaritans requested permission to participate in the rebuilding and were refused, how the first Passover was celebrated by those who had returned, and how Ezra carried out his ministry to the extent of intervening in favor of those who refused to permit foreign wives and giving public readings of the Law. The interpolated story of the three guardsmen depicts a banquet given by Darius I (522–486).

The three young men who guard the great king while he sleeps decide that each of them will secretly write down what he considers to be the most powerful thing on earth. In the morning the king is to decide in the presence of his advisers who has won the contest. Darius opens their answers and gives each an opportunity to justify his opinion. The answers are: wine, the king, and women. The third guardsman, however, who is identified with Zerubbabel, adds a fourth, truth. He emerges victorious; as his reward, he requests permission to return and rebuild the Temple, a request granted by Darius.

Linguistic Problems

In the historical narrative from Josiah to Ezra, we are dealing with a translation of Chronicles and Ezra that diverges from the Greek translation in several respects—including language. In many respects not so closely tied to the Hebrew wording, it uses more appropriate Greek equivalents and also transcribes foreign words differently. For example, Chronicles renders "Passover" as *phasech* (II Chron. 35:8), whereas III Ezra transcribes it as *pascha,* reverting to the Aramaic rather than the Hebrew form. This fact does not require us to conclude that there was an intermediate Aramaic version from which III Ezra was in turn translated; the translator lived among Jews whose ordinary language was Aramaic, and he used more modern terminology than the Torah. His treatment of proper names was somewhat idiosyncratic, but the names may have suffered in the course of subsequent transmission.

The text's fragmentary condition (both a beginning and a conclusion are missing) makes it impossible to say anything definite about its relationship to its parallel. It is reasonable to conclude, however, that the translation of III Ezra dates from a later period than that of the parallel tradition. The story of the three guardsmen is a secondary interpolation, which seems to go back to an Aramaic original that has not been preserved (F. Zimmermann). It is probably a product of Iranian influence, based on a numerical proverb like the proverbs of Agur in Proverbs 30:18-23, 29-31. The Jewish version turns the third guardsman into Zerubbabel; as his reward, he does not receive the royal accolade expected by the circle of guardsmen, but instead is granted permission to rebuild the Temple. We know nothing about the earlier stages of this narrative, which has been turned into a Jewish story by means of interpolation.

Date and Place

With the exception of 3:1–5:4, which is an independent section, III Ezra is a translation—sometimes very free—of texts from the Hebrew Canon. Whether the interpolation, which is written in good Greek, originated with the translator remains uncertain. Such an hypothesis would require that here, free from the necessity of translating a given text, he was able to express himself more freely and thus in better style. In any case, this hypothesis is more likely than the theory that he incorporated a narrative already extant in fixed form. Such a narrative could hardly have provided such an easy transition to the account that follows. Since Josephus bases his presentation in *The Antiquities of the Jews* xi. 11-12 on III Ezra, and since the book emphasizes not only the rebuilding of the Temple after the exile but the regulation of the cultic community and its obligation to obey the Law, we may assume that the latest possible date for the book is the first half of the first century C.E. The story of the guardsmen (before its adaptation to include Zerubbabel) may belong to the fifth century; it probably came into being within the Persian Empire. Borrowed by Jews and altered so as to mention Zerubbabel, it probably achieved its final form at the hands of the translator of III Ezra, who was living in Egypt.

Significance

III Ezra parallels the final chapters of Chronicles and selected portions of Ezra and Nehemiah. The interpolation of the guardsmen story, an example of wisdom literature, is intended to explain the resumption of efforts to rebuild the Temple under Darius. The narrative itself is designed to emphasize the value of wisdom, for wisdom can win the favor of pagan sovereigns and thus contribute to the promotion of Jewish worship.

III. THE PSEUDEPIGRAPHA

A. From the Hellenistic Judaism of Egypt

Letter of Aristeas

Text: Greek—Simon Schard, Basel, 1561; H. St. J. Thackeray in Swete's *Introduction to the Old Testament*, 2nd ed., 1914, pp. 531–606; P. Wendland, *Aristeae Epistula*, 1900.

Translations: Charles (H. T. Andrews), II:83–122; Kautzsch (P. Wendland), II:1–31; Riessler, pp. 193–233, 1277–79; M. Hadas, in *JewApocrLit*, 1951; Kahana (A. Kahana), 2nd ed., 1956.

Monographs: H. G. Meecham, *The Oldest Version of the Bible*, 1932; *idem, The Letter of Aristeas*, 1935; P. Kahle, *The Cairo Geniza*, 1947, pp. 132–37; 2nd ed., 1959, pp. 209–14; B. H. Stricker, *De brief van Aristeas*, 1956; G. Zuntz, "Zum Aristeas-Text," *Philologus*, CII (1958):240–46; *idem,* "Aristeas Studies I: 'The Seven Banquets,'" *JSSt*, IV (1959):21–36; *idem,* "Aristeas Studies II: Aristeas on the Translation of the Torah," *JSSt*, IV (1959):109–26; D. W. Gooding, "Aristeas and Septuagint Origins," *VT*, XIII (1963):357–79; R. Hanhart, "Fragen um die Entstehung der LXX," *VT*, XII (1962):139–63; O. Murray, "Aristeas and Ptolemaic Kingship," *JThSt*, NS XVIII (1967):337–71; L. Rost, "Vermutungen über den Anlaß zur griechischen Übersetzung der Tora," Fs W. Eichrodt, 1970.

BHH, I:127–28 (K. Stendahl); *RGG*, I:596 (W. Michaelis); Eissfeldt, pp. 817–21, 1022–23 (English: 603–6, 773); *IDB*, I:219–21 (G. Zuntz).

Text

The Letter of Aristeas (or "Narrative" [*diêgēsis*] of Aristeas, to use the term by which the document refers to itself in §§ 91 and 322) is preserved in catenae on the Greek translation of the Octateuch. This is natural, since its purpose is to tell how the Septuagint translation came into being. Wendland distinguishes three groups of manuscripts; Thackeray, two. Wendland's third group is represented only by the manuscript Monacensis 9. The manuscript groups are distinguished by their omissions and textual corruptions. All the manuscripts are late, the earliest one dating from the eleventh century.

Contents

The nucleus of the Letter's account tells how Ptolemy II Philadelphus (285–246) at the suggestion of Demetrius of Phaleron, the librarian in charge of the library at Alexandria, sends a delegation to the high priest Eleazar at Jerusalem. They are to request both a Hebrew Torah scroll and a contingent of scholars competent to translate this scroll into Greek. The mission is successful. Seventy-two men, six from each tribe, are selected; upon their arrival in Alexandria they are lodged on the island of Pharos, where they complete their work in seventy-two days. Demetrius assembles the Jewish community of Alexandria and has the translation read aloud; it is approved, and King Ptolemy, informed of the result, rewards the seventy-two scholars and sends them back to Jerusalem with gifts for the high priest Eleazar.

This narrative has been expanded by five additions: (1) the release of the Jewish prisoners who had been deported to Egypt by Ptolemy I Lagi (323–285) (§§ 2-27); (2) a description of the gifts brought by the delegation to the high priest Eleazar (§§ 51-82); (3) a description of Jerusalem and the priesthood (§§ 83-120); (4) a discussion of the Law (§§ 121-71); and (5) table conversations (§§ 187-294).

Author and Date

The author claims to be a Greek—that is, non-Jewish—official in the court of King Ptolemy II Philadelphus (285–246), who was one of the leaders of the mission to the high priest Eleazar and is now reporting what happened to his brother Philocrates. This statement is a fiction. The letter shows clearly that the author was an Alexandrian Jew living considerably later (§§ 28, 182) than the events described. He commits historical errors: Demetrius of Phaleron had been banished around 183 B.C. and had died soon afterwards; he could therefore not have been in office as the administrator of the library. The sea battle against Antigonus near Cos (258 B.C.) was a defeat, not a victory, as § 180 states; and the battle of Andros did not take place until the final year of Ptolemy II's reign—247 B.C. Menedemus is said to have been at the banquet, but it is dubious whether he ever came to Egypt from Eretria (§ 201). These discrepancies are cited by H. T. Andrews. Bickermann, besides citing some earlier observations, adds the demonstration that various idioms in the Letter do not occur until the middle of the second century and later. Examples are the phrase "if it seems good" (§ 32), the title "chief bodyguard(s)" in the plural, and the formula "greetings and salutations." It is therefore best to follow M. Hadas and date the Letter around the year 130 B.C. Wendland assumes that it was composed between 97 and 93 B.C.Willrich and Graetz suggest the reign of Caligula, but this dating is too late, since Aristeas presumes that the island of Pharos is inhabited, whereas Caesar had made it uninhabitable in 63 B.C.

Character

The epistolary form was popular in the ancient world for writing a narrative or report, as the Gospel of Luke and the Acts of the Apostles in the New Testament bear witness. In all three cases the form bears little relationship to the content. In the Letter of Aristeas actually we are dealing with a piece of Jewish propaganda. It sets out to tell how the Pentateuch was translated into Greek, but then uses the account to argue for a favorable attitude toward the Jews on the part of the Ptolemies. This is accomplished by including peripheral matter such as the release of Jewish prisoners of war who were being held as slaves and the table conversations (modeled upon those of the deipnosophists) between Ptolemy II and the seventy-two translators, which provide many occasions for flattery. In addition, the discussions of the priesthood and the Law are meant to produce an understanding of Jewish peculiarities—in part by arousing curiosity—so as to promote the special ethnic and religious status that the author wishes to see protected by privilege under the Ptolemies just as it had been under the Persians.

Sources

One of the sources for the conversations on the philosophy of government appears to be a third-century document called "On Kingship" (*Perì basileías*). Hecateus of Abdera may also have contributed historical material. The author was probably also familiar with Hellenistic popular philosophy.

Significance

The Letter seeks to have the Septuagint recognized as the official translation of the Pentateuch in the Jewish community and by the Ptolemies. The Septuagint is said to have been sanctioned by the community (§§ 308-11), produced at the king's command (§§ 9ff.), and approved by him (§ 312). The Letter also strives to identify Yahweh with Zeus and to show that the Mosaic laws are reasonable and therefore could be recognized by the Greeks. Sin plays a distinctly secondary role (§§ 192, 222-23, 277). The art of statecraft is rectitude and justice—in short—love of humankind (*philanthrōpía*).

Historical Value

As a whole, the account is a fiction. It may be based on the historical reality that certain interests of state (analogous to those that influenced the Persians in the time of Ezra) led the Ptolemies to promote a uniform Greek translation of the Pentateuch for the Jewish community and, once this translation had been made and approved by the community, to declare it binding on the state and on the Jews as a codification of the "laws handed down by the fathers" (*patrǭoi nómoi*).[1] The need for such an action was probably felt as early as the time of Ptolemy II.

Influence

Josephus draws extensively on the Letter of Aristeas in his *Antiquities* xii. 2. Philo likewise was familiar with the document and used it in his *Vita Mosis*. Christian as well as Jewish authors adopted it and, extending it to the entire Canon (Septuagint!), further elaborated the legend. In an appendix to his edition of the Letter, Wendland includes many *testimonia* that illustrate this process of elaboration and exaggeration to the level of the miraculous.

III Maccabees

Text: Greek—Swete, III:709–28; Rahlfs, I:1139–56; LXX Gott, IX/3. Latin—Fritzsche-Grimm (W. Grimm).

Translations: Charles (C. W. Emmet), I:155–73; Kautzsch (E. Kautzsch), I:119–35; Riessler, pp. 682–99; Hartum (E. S. Hartum), 1958; *JewApocrLit* (M. Hadas), 1953; Kahana (T. H. Gaster), 2nd ed., 1956.

Monographs: H. Willrich, "Der historische Kern des III. Makkabäerbuches," *Hermes,* XXXIX (1904):244–58; M. Hadas, "III Maccabees and Greek Romance," *RR,* XIII (1949):155–62; W. Baars, "Eine neue griechische Hand-

---

[1] This translation of the Torah may well have constituted the Magna Charta that made it possible for the Jews to be recognized as a special ethnic group and their worship to be recognized as a *religio licita* in the Hellenistic states, the Roman Empire, and the states arising out of it.

schrift des 3. Makk/Sinai, Cod. gr. 1342, p. 179–85," *VT*, XIII (1963):82–87.

BHH, II:1129 (R. Hanhart); *RGG*, IV:622–23 (U. Luck); Eissfeldt, pp. 788–89, 1021 (English: 581–82, 771); *IDB*, III:210–12 (W. H. Brownlee).

Text

The book, originally written in Greek in a somewhat pretentious style, is found in two uncials (A and V) and a series of minuscules, as well as in the daughter translations. As demonstrated by the word "*de*" in the first sentence, at least one clause was lost at an early date and probably more, since the texts of 1:2 and 2:25 refer to an event already related that is not mentioned in the present text.

Title

The book is generally titled "III Maccabees;" in the minuscules 64 and 236 (Lucianic recension), it is titled *Maccabaica* or *Ptolemaica*, while in minuscule 19 it bears the title "Third Book of the Maccabees." It would be better titled *Ptolemaica*, since the contents go back to the pre-Maccabean period; it recounts events that are said to have taken place in 217 B.C.

Contents

In 217, Ptolemy IV Philopator (221–204) defeated Antiochus III the Great (223–187) at Raphia; now he is visiting the territory he has regained. In Jerusalem he states his desire to enter the Temple, having been granted permission to enter its outer court. Nothing can dissuade him. Despite the pleas of the people of Jerusalem, he insists on carrying out his purpose. An eloquent prayer to God brings about convulsions and paralysis so that his bodyguards have to carry him away. Having recovered and returned to Egypt, he persecutes the Egyptian Jews and plans their total destruction. He has the Jews throughout Egypt arrested and brought into the stadium at Alexandria. He commands the chief of five hundred elephants to drive the elephants into a frenzy with incense and unmixed wine and loose them on the assembled Jews upon his signal. The first chance is lost when the king oversleeps, the second when God makes the king totally forget his purpose. On the third occasion, in response to the prayer of a certain Eleazar, two shining angels appear before the king and his soldiers, so that the elephants turn upon the forces of the king. Now the king changes his mind, gives the Jews a banquet, honors them, and lets them return home—first giving them permission to slay apostate Jews. The festival celebration becomes a memorial festival.

Genre

III Maccabees is an historically motivated festival legend similar to Esther or the earlier festival legends of Passover and the Feast of Booths. This legend differs from Esther in its occasionally bombastic style and its emphasis on the supernatural intervention of the angels (6:18).

Historicity

Although it is likely that there was some historical occasion for the celebration of the festival in Alexandria (it is mentioned also by Josephus), and although the description of the historical events at the battle of Raphia is accurate and the journey to Jerusalem appears reasonable, the rest of the story is highly unlikely. At the very least it is highly exaggerated. Furthermore, in *Contra Apionem* ii. 5 Josephus ascribes the attempt to take all the Jews captive and have them stand naked in readiness to be trampled by elephants to Ptolemy VII Physcon (146–117). It is naturally possible to draw the conclusion that the history of the Jews in Egypt includes situations in which the very existence of Jews was endangered and even that on some occasion command was given to have certain Jews, or the Jewish population of one or more cities, trampled by elephants. But there is no certain evidence of such an event. The permission to slay apostate Jews is probably wholly legendary, although it is likely that such illegal executions were occasionally carried out (cf. D. von Dobschütz, *Paulus und die jüdische Torapolizei,* 1968, pp. 42 ff.).

Author, Place, and Date

The author was a Greek-speaking Jew from Egypt, probably from Alexandria, who recorded the festival legend of a joyous feast. He is one of those who would prefer to maintain their ancestral customs and eradicate the apostate. The book probably dates from the last third of the first century B.C.

Significance

The book gives us an insight into the fears and hopes of the Jews in Egypt. The festival legend serves to bolster faith in Yahweh's aid in times of peril. The angelology of the book is noteworthy.

IV Maccabees

Text: Greek—Swete, III:720–62; Rahlfs, I:1157–84; Fritzsche, 351–86.

Translations: Charles (R. B. Townshend), II:653–85; Kautzsch, (A. Deissmann), II:149–77; Riessler, pp. 700–28; *JewApocrLit* (M. Hadas), 1953; Kahana (A. Schur), 2nd ed., 1956.

Commentaries: A. Dupont-Sommer, 1939.

Monographs: H. Dörrie, *Passio SS. Machabaeorum; die antike lateinische Übersetzung des IV. Makkabäerbuches,* AGA, II/22, 1938; P. Staples, "The Unused Lever? A Study on the Possible Literary Influence of the Greek Maccabean Literature in the NT," *ModChm,* IX (1966):218–24.

BHH, II:1129–30 (R. Hanhart); *RGG,* IV:622–23 (U. Luck); Eissfeldt, pp. 831–34, 1023 (English: 613–15, 774); *IDB,* III:212–15 (W. H. Brownlee).

Text

The three majuscules Sinaiticus, A, and V, as well as a series of minuscules, include the complete text. The book is

also preserved in the setting of certain Josephus manuscripts. A Syriac translation has been edited by R. L. Bensly
on the basis of nine manuscripts and published with an
introduction. It has also been translated by W. E. Barnes.
No Old Latin version is extant. In 1517, Erasmus dedicated
a Latin paraphrase (*Unius dieculae opellam*) to Helias
Marcaeus, moderator of the Maccabean Collegium at
Cologne.

Title

The majuscules call the book IV Maccabees. In Josephus
manuscripts it usually takes its title from its contents,
"Concerning the Superiority of Reason" (*Perì autokrátoros
logismoū*). In editions of Josephus we find still other titles,
such as "Concerning the Rational Logos" (*Perì sốphronos
lógou*) and "The Book of Josephus upon the Maccabees"
(*Iōsíppou eis toùs Makkabaíous biblíon*).

Contents

The author's purpose is to examine a "wholly
philosophical question"—can religious reason of her own
accord become mistress over the passions? At the same
time, he counsels men for their own benefit to hold fast to
philosophy. He brings all the forces of rhetoric to bear on
the question. In chapters 1–3, he takes up particular ethical
problems and illustrates the power of reason through
examples taken from the conduct of Jacob, Joseph, and
David. Then he moves on to the history of the recent past,
recounting the intrigues of Simon, who envied Onias the
office of high priest, telling of the attempt of Apollodorus
to enter the Temple (instigated by the order of Antiochus
Epiphanes), of the replacement of Simon with Jason
(3:19–4:26), and of the persecution of the Jews by
Antiochus, using the examples of Eleazar (cf. II Macc.
6:18-31) and of the mother and her seven sons (cf. II
Macc. 7). In spite of torture and threatened execution,
reason led these faithful souls to maintain their fear of God
and thus remain superior to the threats of the king; at the

same time, they became models for the people (5:1–17:6). The striking conclusion begins with an imaginary memorial inscription ascribing the deliverance of the nation to the death of these sacrificial victims; there follows a call to emulate them. Then the mother addresses her sons, pointing out to them how careful she had been to observe the Law and the traditional customs of the fathers. The book ends with a hymn in praise of God, who took vengeance on Antiochus for the execution of the victims but received the victims of his tyranny into "the company of the fathers once they had received pure and immortal souls" (17:7–18:24; following A. Deissmann in Kautzsch, p. 177).

Genre and Unity

Freudenthal suggested that the book was an early synagogue sermon. This proposal has been attacked on the grounds that synagogue sermons in late Judaism always took a biblical text as their point of departure. It is therefore better to follow Norden in calling the document a later form of the diatribe, one that presents its subject matter in the form of a sermon. This would mean that we are dealing with a genre common to late Greek philosophy. It is being utilized by an author highly dependent on Stoic philosophy to encourage his Jewish compatriots to have the courage to face martyrdom.

Two passages in the tractate raise problems of literary criticism. Verses 5 and 6 of chapter 1 seem more appropriate in the context of 2:24–3:1, since they anticipate a question to be discussed later and interrupt the structure of the introduction. The repetition of the mother's speech in 18:6-19 is awkward following 18:6. But it is difficult to find any better location for this rather abruptly introduced oration, which is of interest for the light it throws on the domestic education of children. It must be explained either as a recapitulation or as a postscript that found its way into the text at an early date. Its appropriateness to the diatribe must be acknowledged.

JUDAISM OUTSIDE THE HEBREW CANON

Author

The author is a Jew so thoroughly conversant with Greek that he is even able to compose an original work that is formally irreproachable and to make effective use of an extensive vocabulary. He exhibits a familiarity with Greek philosophy, especially with that of the Stoa, and has rhetorical talent. At the same time, however, he remains faithful to the Law, refusing to abandon, mitigate, or reinterpret the patriarchal traditions. In particular, he is not influenced by Philo's allegorizing approach. He probably lived in Alexandria, not Antioch. Since the Temple is apparently still standing, the year A.D. 70 must probably be taken as *terminus ante quem.* The first half of the first century C.E. might be suggested as the time when the book was written.

Significance

IV Maccabees shows how a Hellenistically educated Jew could use his education to support his fidelity to his ancestral Law. The notion that the philosophical virtues of Plato and the Stoa could reinforce a readiness to fulfill the Law was a misunderstanding possible only because religion had to a large extent been reduced to law and fulfillment of the law identified with fear of God. The substitution of the belief in the immortality of the soul for hope in the resurrection of the flesh to a life upon a renewed earth in the day of salvation, to be sure, marked a total conversion to Greek thought.

Slavonic Enoch

Text: S. Novaković, *Starine*, Zagreb, XVI (1884):67–81; A. Vaillant, *Le livre des secrets d'Hénoch, texte slave et traduction française,* 1952.

Translations: Charles (N. Forbes and R. H. Charles), II:425–69; Kautzsch (G. Beer), II:218, note a; Riessler, pp. 452–73; N. Bonwetsch, *Die Bücher der Geheimnisse Henochs,* 1922; Kahana (A. Kahana), 2nd ed., 1956.

Monographs: A. Rubinstein, "Observations on the Slavonic Book of Henoch," *JJSt*, XIII (1962):1–21; F. Repp, "Textkritische Untersuchungen zum Henoch-Apokryph des cod. slav. 125 der österreich. Nationalbibliothek," *Wiener Slavistisches Jahrbuch*, X (1963):58–68; N. A. Meščerskij, *Traces of Literary Remains of Qumran in Old Slavonic and Ancient Russian Literature* (in Russian), 1963; *idem*, "Zur Quellenfrage des slav. Henoch," *KratSInAz*, LXXXVI (1965):72–78; *idem*, "Zur Textgeschichte des slav. Henoch," *VizVrem*, XXIV (1964):91-108.

BHH, II:693 (B. Reicke); *RGG*, III:224-25 (O. Plöger); Eissfeldt, pp. 843–44, 1024 (English: 622–23, 774).

Text

Slavonic Enoch has been preserved in two versions—a longer South Russian version in a manuscript from the second half of the seventeenth century, published in 1880 by A. Popov, and a shorter version, itself incomplete, in a Serbian manuscript belonging to the public library in Belgrade, published in 1884 by S. Novakovič. Both derive from a common Greek tradition (cf. the derivation of the name "Adam" from the intial letters of *anatolē, dýsis, árktos,* and *mēsembría*). Whether a Hebrew original should be hypothesized for certain sections is uncertain but reasonable in view of the quotations from the book in the Testaments of the Twelve Patriarchs (Test. Levi 14, 16; Test. Judah 18; Test. Dan 5; Test. Napht. 4) and other contemporary documents.

Contents

The book begins with an account of Enoch's journey through the ten heavens (originally perhaps only seven heavens) (1-21). Enoch then has an audience with God himself, who instructs Enoch about the process of creation from its beginning *ex nihilo* to the creation of man and about the duration of the world (seven thousand years plus a millennium) (22-23). God then has two angels escort Enoch back to earth for a short period so that he can instruct his children about the future destiny of the world and of mankind (34-38). Enoch recounts the mysteries of heaven he has observed, then adds an exhortation and the command to disseminate his books (39-54). The book concludes with a farewell discourse and an account of Enoch's ascension.

Relationship to Ethiopic Enoch

It is clear that we are dealing with one of the further elaborations of the Enoch tradition—like that represented by the Ethiopic Book of Enoch. The common motifs, however, such as the journey through the heavens and the interest in astronomical and meteorological questions, very early began their independent development, so that the details differ markedly. Interpolations have also been inserted in Slavonic Enoch, probably by a Christian hand; and the book was handed down in the West, not in Africa.

Place and Date

The association with the West is all the more remarkable in that the Greek recension of the book (which represents at least an important stage in the formation of the tradition, if not the crucial initial stage) undoubtedly came into being in Egypt within the circle of Hellenistic Jews who were influenced but not overwhelmed by the intellectual milieu represented by Philo. Since the author had before him Sirach, Ethiopic Enoch, and the Wisdom of Solomon, but states the Temple was still standing (51, 59, 61, 62, 68), the work should probably be dated in the first half of the first century C.E. Its final form is due to a Christian revision in the Eastern Church dating from the seventh century.

Significance

The book illustrates a Diaspora piety interested in the Jerusalem cult, with particular emphasis on love of one's neighbor.

112

Sibylline Oracles

Text: C. Alexandre, *Oracula Sibyllinam* 1841–56, 2nd ed. 1869; J. Geffcken, *Oracula Sibyllina*, 1902; A. M. Kurfess, *Sibyllinische Weissagungen; Urtext und Übersetzung*, 1951.

Translations: Charles (H. C. O. Lanchester), II:368–408; Kautzsch (F. Blass), II:177–217; Riessler, pp. 1014–45, 1326–28; Kahana (J. Reider), 2nd ed., 1956; Hennecke-Schneemelcher (A. Kurfess), 1964, pp. 498-528.

Monographs: W. L. Kinter, "Prophetess and Fay: A Study of the Ancient and Mediaeval Tradition of the Sibyl," dissertation, Columbia, 1958; R. Dornseiff, "Die sibyllinischen Orakel in der augusteischen Dichtung," in *Römische Dichtung der augusteischen Zeit*, 1960; R. Bloch, "La divination romaine et les Livres sibyllins," *RÉLat*, XL (1962):118–20; B. Noack, "Are the Essenes Referred to in the Sibylline Oracles?" *ST*, XVII (1963):90–93.

BHH, III:1779–80 (P. Geoltrain); *RGG*, VI:14–15 (F. C. Grant); Eissfeldt, pp. 834–36, 1023–24 (English: 615–17, 774); *IDB*, III:343.

Text

The Sibylline Oracles have been preserved in ten manuscripts of the fourteenth and fifteenth centuries, some of which contain only individual books. These represent three textual groups: Ω, Φ, and Ψ. There are two additional manuscripts containing excerpts as well as many quotations from the Fathers (R. H. Charles). They are written in late Attic Greek, in hexameters that are often imperfect; the language echoes that of Homer and the Ionic epics.

Title

The Sibyllines (*Tà Sibýlleia* [*grámmata*]) are a pseudepigraphon capitalizing on the esteem accorded to the name of the pagan Sibyls by the Greeks and Romans. "Sybyls" was the name or appellation for inspired women "who, in a state of ecstasy, gave an intimation of coming events,

113

usually unpleasant and terrifying; this they did on their own initiative, without being asked or having any association with a specific oracular shrine" (A. M. Kurfess). Much evidence suggests the legend was of Iranian origin. At first there was one wandering Sibyl; later she was joined by others, up to a total of ten. Especially famous were the Sibyl of Erythrae in Ionia and the Sibyl of Cumae in southern Italy, who sold the three Sibylline books to the Roman King Tarquinius Priscus; these were guarded in the Capitol by ten men, later fifteen (*quindecim viri sacris faciundis*), until 82 B.C., when they perished with the burning of the Capitol. The second century B.C. witnessed the beginning of a large-scale fabrication of pseudo-Sibylline texts, especially in Hellenistic territory, above all in Ptolemaic Egypt. The Jews and later the Christians made use of these texts for missionary and apologetic purposes. Late texts of this type are preserved in the Sibylline Oracles.

Extent

The Sibylline Oracles comprised fifteen books, of which 1–8 and 11–14 have been preserved. Books 3–5, along with three fragments preserved in *Theophilus ad Autolycum*, exhibit Jewish authorship or editing. Books 3 and 5 in particular are composed of quite diverse materials.

Contents

Threats of catastrophe up to and including the end of the world alternate with attacks on idolatry, on the Ptolemies, on the Seleucids, and on the Romans. References to the Deluge, the Tower of Babylon, and historical events of the past are interspersed with exhortations and encouragement.

Date

The individual sections derive from different periods. The earliest date from the early Maccabean period (e.g., 3:46ff.); the latest date from the Christian Era (e.g., 4:128-29, 143-44, dating from A.D. 76). The Jewish oracles were taken over by the Christian church at an early date, probably because of their Old Testament content, their rejection of idolatry, and their hostility toward Rome. With this, the Jewish community lost interest in these documents. However, the increase in Christian fabrication of sayings attributed to the Sibyls and the frequent citation of these sayings down to the Middle Ages and beyond (cf. the Sibyls of Michelangelo in the Sistine Chapel) attest their popularity.

Author

We are probably dealing with several authors, all presumably writing in Egypt (Alexandria). They, in order to justify their use of a figure borrowed from the Greeks, rejected Homer as a forger of the Sibylline idiom and made the Sibyl the daughter-in-law of Noah (3:826).

Significance

The Jewish Sibyllines belong to the period of controversy with Hellenism and missionary activity among the Greeks. Just as the Greeks were turned into interpreters of Jewish laws and doctrines, so pagan prophecies and wisdom were projected as expressions of Jewish ideas. The Old Testament taught men to think of Yahweh as the instigator of disasters and natural catastrophes. By attributing similar statements to the Sibyl, the author hoped to show that her philosophies did not differ in principle from the teachings of the Old Testament. The Jewish attack on the Romans as a common enemy was an attempt to win over the Greeks, who were in the same position as they. The same trains of thought are found in the writings of the apologists.

B. From Syria

Greek Apocalypse of Baruch

Text: Greek—M. R. James, *Apocrypha anecdota*, II (1897):li-lxxi, 84–94; J.-C. Picard, *Apocalypsis Baruchi graece*, 1967.

Slavonic: S. Novaković, *Starine*, Zagreb, XVIII (1886):203–9.

Translations (of the Slavonic text): English—M. R. James, *Apocrypha anecdota*, II (1897):95–102; Charles (H. M. Hughes), II:527-41. German—N. G. Bonwetsch, "Das slavisch erhaltene Baruch-Buch," *NGG*, 1896, pp. 91–101; Kautzsch (V. Ryssel), II:446–57; Riessler, pp. 40–54, 1269–70; Kahana (E. S. Artom), 2nd ed., 1956.

Monographs: W. Lüdtke, "Beiträge zu slavischen Apokryphen," ZAW, XXXI (1911):218–35.

BHH, I:203 (M. Weise); *RGG*, I:902–3 (O. Plöger); Eissfeldt, pp. 854–55 (English: 630–31).

Text

This Apocalypse of Baruch is preserved only in a Greek manuscript from the sixteenth century. Discovered in the British Museum (Add. 10073) by E. C. Butler in 1896, it was published by M. R. James in 1897. There is also an abbreviated Slavonic recension from a sixteenth century manuscript, which was published by S. Novaković in 1886. This is probably the work referred to by Origen in his *De principiis* ii. 3. 6: "Denique etiam Baruch prophetae librum in assertione huius testimonium vocant, quod ibi de septem mundis vel caelis evidentius indicatur."

Title

The Greek manuscript bears a double title: first, *Diēgēsis kai apokálypsis Baroúch . . .* , second, *Apokálypsis Baroúch. . . .* M. R. James, who first published the manuscript, called it *Apocalypsis Baruchi tertia graece.*

Contents

Baruch, alongside the Kidron, laments the destruction of Jerusalem by Nebuchadnezzar. He is comforted by an angel, who promises to show him the secrets of God. The angel thereupon conducts Baruch through five heavens, telling him the dimensions of each and pointing out and explaining their inhabitants. These include (in the third heaven) the sun chariot, accompanied by the phoenix that captures the rays of the sun with its wings, and (in the fifth heaven) the archangel Michael, who bears the works of the righteous into the presence of God. Then the angel accompanies Baruch back to earth. There is no trace of eschatological exaggeration or messianic expectation in the book.

Unity and Form

We can hardly be dealing with the work in its original form. In the first place, 4:9-15 is undoubtedly a Christian interpolation intended to annul the curse on the grape as a plant secretly planted by Satan in Paradise by referring to the significance of wine as an element of the Eucharist. In the second place, the original conclusion is missing. If the passage from Origen cited above does indeed refer to this Apocalypse, it spoke originally of seven heavens; whereas now it mentions only five. Elaboration of the passage about Michael as the mediator of the good deeds performed by the devout probably accounts for the change in ending. A similar passage occurs in the Apocalypse of Paul—whether this latter Apocalypse or an antecedent tradition was borrowed by the Apocalypse of Baruch cannot be determined.

From the perspective of form criticism, we are dealing with an example of revelation literature, which, under the guise of a journey through the heavens, attempts to answer meteorological and eschatological questions.

Significance

On the one hand, this document, like Enoch, satisfies religious curiosity. On the other hand, it has an unmistakable ethical and didactic undertone intended to gratify the hearts of those who hear how the godless suffer and the righteous are glorified. Thus the document is using revelation of hidden secrets to call on the reader to maintain his moral standards. A Christian interpolation rejects the original condemnation of wine, at least for use in the Lord's Supper.

117

JUDAISM OUTSIDE THE HEBREW CANON

C. From Palestinian Pharisaism

Psalms of Solomon

Text: Greek—Swete, III:765–87; Rahlfs, II:471–89; Fritzsche, pp. 569–89; O. von Gebhardt, *Psalmoi Solomôntos,* 1895. Syriac—J. R. Harris and A. Mingana, *The Odes and Psalms of Solomon,* 2 vols., 1916–20. Retranslation into Hebrew—W. Frankenberg, *Die Datierung der Psalmen Salomos,* 1896, pp. 66–77.

Translations: Charles (G. B. Gray), II:625–52; Kautzsch (R. Kittel), II:127–48; Riessler, pp. 881–902, 1323–24; Kahana (M. Stein), 2nd ed., 1956.

Monographs: J. Efron, "The Psalms of Solomon; the Hasmonean Decline and Christianity" [Hebrew], *Tsiyon,* XXX/1–2 (1965):1–46; M. de Jonge, *De toekomsverwachting in de Psalmen van Salomo,* 1965; K. Koch, "Der Schatz im Himmel," in *Festschrift H. Thielicke,* 1968, pp. 47–60.

BHH, III:1520–21 (M. S. Enslin); *RGG,* V:1342–43 (H. Braun); Eissfeldt, pp. 826–31 (English: 610–13); *IDB,* III:958–60.

Text

The early Christian lists of canonical books sometimes included the eighteen psalms ascribed to Solomon among the Apocrypha and other times included them among the Antilegomena. Until the seventeenth century, however, they were considered lost. Rediscovered by the Augsburg librarian David Hoeschel, they were first published by the Jesuit John Louis de la Cerda in 1626. Today we know of eight Greek manuscripts from the eleventh through the fifteenth centuries and three Syriac manuscripts, none of which are quite complete. The Hebrew original on which both versions are based is still missing. The Greek version is a direct translation; the Syriac, as K. G. Kuhn has shown, also drew on the Greek version, which derives in turn from the Hebrew text.

Title and Compass

The title "Psalms of Solomon" was probably given to this collection by a compiler in order to distinguish it from the canonical Psalms of David, while at the same time, however, associating the collection with the name of a famous king. The text does not contain any even indirect reference to Solomon. The collection comprises eighteen psalms that formally resemble the canonical Psalms; like the hymns from Qumran, however, they contain a marked element of reflection.

Author, Date, and Place

The psalms may be the work of a single author. It is less likely that poems of several authors dating from about the same period with similar theological views were brought together by a compiler. The compiler or an early editor ascribed them to Solomon. The theological stance is largely a product of Pharisaism; in any case, it differs markedly from that of the Qumran sect. Since historical allusions in Psalms 2, 8, and 17 portray the rule of Pompey in Palestine (after 63 B.C.) and his death at Casius east of the Pelusic branch of the Nile (48 B.C.), the Psalms can be dated to the second half of the first century B.C. Earlier attempts to date their origin in the Maccabean period encountered difficulties.

Genre and Contents

The Old Testament psalm forms of hymn and lament are also found in the Psalms of Solomon, albeit usually overgrown with passages of reflection and description, and often combined. Wisdom psalms like Psalm 1 of the canonical book also turn up, as 4:23 ff., 6, 10, and 14 illustrate. In content, the Psalms of Solomon describe the devout adherent of the Law and the wicked man who departs from the Law and depict each of their fates; they tell of the unexpected judgment brought upon the entire nation by Pompey, whose soldiers desecrated the sanctuary and carried off Jewish prisoners westwards, and look forward to the dawning age of salvation.

Affinities

The Psalms of Solomon are derivative from the canonical book of Psalms. The question of whether, like the latter, they were employed in the public cult or in the worship of a particular group cannot be determined with certainty, despite the technical terminology in 8:1, 15:1, 17:1, 17:29, and 18:9, since these phrases may be interpolations by a compiler editing the whole collection. The structure and diction of the Eleventh Psalm derive from Baruch 5:1-9 (W. Pesch).

Significance

The Psalms of Solomon give us an insight into the religious milieu of the second half of the first century B.C.—more precisely, into the thought of a group closely related to the Pharisees, whose members were devoted to the Temple, though without particular emphasis on the worship of the Temple, and its sacrificial cult. The way of life that pleases God is faithful obedience to the Law; but the approach is not identical with the separatist legalism of the Qumran community, from whom the group also differs in the reduced importance it attaches to Old Testament prophecy.

IV Ezra

Text: Latin—*Vulgata*, II:1931-74. Retranslation into Greek—A. Hilgenfeld, *Messias Judaeorum*, 1869, pp. 36-113. All texts, with a German or Latin translation of the Oriental versions, will be found in B. Violet, *Die Esra-Apokalypse (IV Esra)*, I, 1910; R. P. Blake, "The Georgian Version of Fourth Esdras from the Jerusalem Manuscript," *HThR*, XIX (1926):299-375; *idem*, "The Georgian Text of Fourth Esdras from the Athos Manuscript," *HThR*, XXII (1929):57-105.

Translations: Charles (G. H. Box), II:542–624; Kautzsch (H. Gunkel), II:331–401; Riessler, pp. 255–309, 1282–85; Hammershaimb (B. Noack), 1953; Kahana (A. Kahana), 2nd ed., 1956; B. Violet, *Die Apokalypsen des Esra und des Baruch in deutscher Gestalt*, 1924. Commentaries: W. O. E. Oesterley (WC), 1933. Monographs: J. Bloch, "Was There a Greek Version of the Apocalypse of Ezra?" *JQR*, XLVI (1955/56):309–20; *idem*, "The Ezra-Apocalypse, Was it Written in Hebrew, Greek, or Aramaic?" *JQR*, XLVIII (1957/58):279–84; *idem*, "Some Christological Interpolations in the Ezra-Apocalypse," *HThR*, LI (1958):87–94; F. Zimmermann, "Underlying Documents of IV Ezra," *JQR*, LI (1960/61):107–34; M. Stone, "Features of the Eschatology of IV Esdras," dissertation, Harvard, 1964; *idem*, "Some Features of the Armenian Version of IV Ezra," *Muséon*, LXXIX (1966):387–400; *idem*, "Paradise in 4 Ezra IV. 8 and VII. 36, VIII. 52," *JJSt*, XVII (1966):85–88; G. Reese, "Die Geschichte Israels in der Auffassung des frühen Judentums; eine Untersuchung der Geschichtsdarstellung des 4. Esrabuches," dissertation, Heidelberg, WS 1967–68; M. E. Stone, "Manuscripts and Readings of Armenian IV Ezra," *Textus*, VI (1968):48–61; K. Koch, "Der Schatz im Himmel," in *Festschrift H. Thielicke*, 1968, pp. 47–60; W. Harnisch, *Verhängnis und Verheißung der Geschichte; Untersuchungen zum Zeit- und Geschichtsverständnis im 4. Buch Esra und in der syrischen Baruchapokalypse*, FRLANT 97, 1969.

BHH, I:442–43 (L. H. Silberman); *RGG*, II:697–99 (O. Plöger); Eissfeldt, pp. 846–49 (English: 624–27); *IDB*, II:140–42.

Text

The book is extant in Latin, Syriac, Ethiopic, Arabic, Armenian, Sahidic, and Georgian translations, which in turn go back (via a lost Greek translation, preserved only in quotations from the Greek Fathers) to an original probably written in Hebrew rather than Aramaic (R. H. Charles). The Latin translation is even included as an appendix to the Vulgate, albeit sandwiched between two initial chapters (also referred to as V Ezra) and two final chapters (also referred to as VI Ezra), but is missing a section that should be inserted between 7:35 and 7:36, which was lost when a leaf was removed from Codex Sangermanensis (written in 822). Almost all the Latin manuscripts follow this mutilated codex; only six (the most important of which is the ninth-century Codex Ambianensis) include this section, which is preserved in the Syriac translation. The Syriac text is preserved only in a sixth-century biblical manuscript of the Ambrosian Library in Milan. The Ethiopic translation is extant in several manuscripts. Two complete and independent Arabic translations are known; one is preserved at Oxford, the other in the Vatican. Excerpts and fragments of the latter are also found at Oxford and Paris. The Armenian translation is very free. According to M. E. Stone, it is based on a lost Greek original with Christian revisions. Only fragments of the Sahidic and Georgian translations have been preserved.

Title

The Latin manuscripts introduce the book as IV Ezra (*Esdrae liber IV*), with separate titles (V and VI Ezra) for the chapters 1–2 and 15–16 added as a framework in the Christian Era. Clement of Alexandria cites the title in Greek as *Esdras ho prophētēs* ("Esdras the Prophet"); Ambrose borrows this title.

Contents

We will deal only with chapters 3–14, written by a Jewish author. They contain seven "visions"; but the first three are dialogues, and the last is an account of how an angel commissions Ezra, with the aid of five men, to write down what he is about to hear in ninety-four books, seventy of which are to remain secret.

The first dialogue (3:1–5:19) discusses the origins of the world's sin and suffering and ends with a comforting vision of the rapidly approaching end. The second (5:20–6:34) examines the question of why God has abandoned his own beloved people to the Gentiles, referring to God's secret plan for the world and the approach of the end, which will reveal that plan. The third dialogue (6:35–9:25) devotes itself first of all to the question of why Israel does not already possess the world (since it is already theirs by promise), looks upon this world as a passage, speaks of the fate of sinners and of the judgment of the world, describes the sevenfold agony and sevenfold joy of the intermediate state, rejects all possibility of intercession at the judgment, and struggles with the problem of reconciling God's mercy with the destruction of the sinful. It concludes with an admonition that Ezra, who is destined for eternal bliss, would do better to think about his own future than to brood over the lot of sinners, which they deserve.

Then follow the three visions. The first (9:26–10:60) depicts a woman in mourning and describes her suffering. She is transformed into a glorious city, the Jerusalem of the day of salvation. The next vision (11:1–12:51)—the fifth of the whole series—illustrates the course of future history by means of an eagle emerging from the sea and its bodily proportions. The sixth vision depicts one like a man rising out of the sea, who, with the clouds of heaven at the head of a great army, attacks his foes with a stream of fire until they are reduced to smoke and ashes. The seventh vision (14:1–50) records the commission, described above, to write the twenty-four canonical books and the seventy secret books.

Unity

The book with its seven "visions" claims to have been written in Babylon by Shealtiel, also called Ezra, in the thirtieth year after the fall of the city. The father of Zerubbabel, mentioned in Ezra 3:2 and elsewhere, for whom the date and location ring true, has been confused with Ezra, who belongs to the fifth century. This confusion suggests that material of diverse origin has been brought together. The vision of the eagle, for example, which recalls Daniel and expands on the Daniel passage, experienced a lengthy history before it was incorporated here. The vision of the son of man is also intrusive, as is above all the final vision with its commission to Ezra to write the twenty-four canonical books and an additional seventy secret books with the assistance of five men. R. H. Charles hypothesizes the work of a redactor who combined the sections just mentioned with an Apocalypse of Shealtiel comprising the first four visions; it is more likely, however, that the author revised and assembled the earlier materials.

Author and Date

The author was neither Shealtiel nor Ezra, but a Jew who lived around the end of the first century C.E. He was still influenced by one of the destructions of Jerusalem, the shock of which he had not yet overcome; this destruction cannot be that of 587 B.C., but is probably the catastrophe of A.D. 70. If so, the "thirtieth" year—probably selected with reference to Ezra 1:1—can be understood only as a round-number estimate; for the vision of the eagle, interpreted (as it probably should be) as applying to the Roman Empire, would point to the reign of Domitian (A.D. 81–96). It is impossible to say with certainty whether the author lived in Jerusalem or perhaps among the Jewish Diaspora in Rome. There is no reason to rule out Jerusalem; much evidence, especially the universal perspective, suggests Rome. There is no trace of any influence from Egyptian Judaism or from the Qumran community.

Significance

The book shows us a Judaism for which the old ideals of precise fulfillment of the Law and self-righteous seclusion have been shattered; Judaism now sees itself as a tiny minority chosen by God and confronting the rest of mankind, whom God has rejected. The question is therefore not about the righteousness of God, but about his mercy. This more open Judaism, transcending the limits of particularistic nationalism, no longer looks upon its own catastrophe as merely a national disaster, as does the author of Lamentations; nor, like Job, does it consider its own suffering reason to question God's righteousness. Such a Judaism should hardly be sought within the narrow confines of Palestine. Unlike the author of Lamentations or of Job, the author of IV Ezra had eschatological hope in the coming age of salvation as an answer; but in this respect, too, he is concerned with the expectations of all mankind, not the coming of salvation for his own nation. Thus the book in many ways occupies a unique position, which is not diminished by the fact that its ideas are borrowed in part by the Syriac Apocalypse of Baruch.

Syriac Apocalypse of Baruch

Text: Syriac—A. M. Ceriani, *Monumenta sacra et profana*, V/2 (1871):113–80; R. Graffin, *Patrologia syriaca*, I/2 (1907):1056–1306 (M. Kmosko). Greek—Oxyrhynchus Fragment in Charles, II:487–90; B. P. Grenfell and A. S. Hunt, *The Oxyrhynchus Papyri*, III (1903):3–7 (#403).

Translations: Charles (R. H. Charles), II:470–526; Kautzsch (V. Ryssel), II:404–46; Riessler, pp. 55–113, 1270–72; B. Violet, *Die Apokalypsen des Esra und des Baruch in deutscher Gestalt*, 1924; Kahana (A. Kahana), 2nd ed., 1956.

Monographs: F. Zimmermann, "Textual Observations on the Apocalypse of Baruch," *JThSt*, XL (1939):151–56; K. Koch, "Der Schatz im Himmel," in *Festschrift H. Thielicke*, 1968, pp. 47–60.

BHH, I:202–3 (M. Weise); *RGG*, I:901–3 (O. Plöger); Eissfeldt, pp. 850–53, 1024 (English: 627–30, 775); *IDB*, I:361–62.

Text

The complete text of this Apocalypse is preserved in a sixth-century Syriac biblical manuscript from Milan (Codex Ambrosianus B 21 Inf. fol. 265b-267b). It was discovered by A. M. Ceriani, who published a Latin translation in

1866, the Syriac text in 1881, and a facsimile of the text in 1883. Chapters 78–86, the letter of Baruch to the nine and a half tribes, have been part of the Syriac Bible since the beginning. A critical edition of them was published by R. H. Charles in 1896 on the basis of manuscripts from Milan, London, and Oxford, together with readings from Walton's Polyglott and the Paris Polyglott. A fragment of a Greek translation is found in the *Oxyrhynchus Papyri* (III:37), from the fourth century, containing 12:1-5; 13:1-2, 11-12; and 14:1-3.

This Apocalypse was originally composed in Hebrew. According to its own statement, the Syriac translation was made from a Greek translation. The Hebrew original has been lost; the Oxyrhynchus fragment is all that is left of the Greek translation. The single manuscript containing the Syriac daughter translation is therefore the only witness to the whole text. It, too, appears not to have preserved the exact original tradition; according to 77:12, 17, and 19, Baruch was to write two letters, one to the nine and a half tribes beyond the Euphrates, the other to the two and a half tribes in Babylon. Only the former is preserved. R. H. Charles has suggested that the latter is identical with portions of the book of Baruch in the Apocrypha, specifically Baruch 1:1-3; 3:9–4:29. This would imply that this latter letter was more widely recognized by the church than the rest of the book, including the letter to the nine and a half tribes, and was therefore handed down separately in the Greek, Latin, and Syriac churches.

Title

In the manuscript, the book bears the title "The Book of the Revelation of Baruch ben Neriah," translated from Greek into Syriac.

Contents

The book is divided into seven sections.

1) Chapters 1–12. In the twenty-fifth year of Jeconiah, God announces to Baruch that Jerusalem will fall the next

day. Angels bring this to pass, and the Chaldeans occupy the fallen city. At God's command, Baruch remains in the city, while Jeremiah goes to Babylon with the exiles.

2) Chapters 13–20. After Baruch fasts for seven days, God reveals to him that judgment will befall the Gentiles, too, and shows him the fate of the righteous and of the unrighteous. Finally God commands him to fast for seven more days.

3) Chapters 21–34. Baruch prepares by means of prayer and fasting to receive a new revelation, which answers his question about the judgment to befall the godless, which will extend over the whole earth and precede the appearance of the Messiah. Then Baruch summons the elders and informs them that Zion is to be rebuilt but will shortly thereafter be destroyed a second time, whereupon a glorious period of reconstruction will follow.

4) Chapters 35–46. Baruch laments over the ruins of the holy of holies; sleep overcomes him, and in a dream he sees a great forest in a valley surrounded by rocks. A vine begins to grow. From beneath it issues a stream that grows until it brings down both rocks and forest, all except for a single cedar. The cedar finally falls victim to flames, and the vine flourishes. God interprets the dream vision, explaining that the forest symbolizes the series of world empires from Daniel, while the vine signifies the Anointed One, whose kingdom will finally stand alone and exist forever. Baruch is commissioned to exhort his people.

5) Chapters 47–52. Having fasted and prayed, Baruch receives a revelation about conditions in the final days of distress and about the bodies the resurrected will have in the future.

6) Chapters 53–76. Baruch sees a cloud rising up from the sea, which sends forth twelve rainstorms, dark and bright alternating. They are followed by a great dark rain and finally bright lightning. The angel Ramiel interprets these rains as signifying the periods of history from the Fall to the return from Babylon; these will be followed by the afflictions of the eschaton and the bright lightning of the

Messiah and his age. Baruch gives thanks, whereupon he is told that he will be transported to a high mountain, which he must climb in forty days.

7) Chapters 77–87. Baruch assembles the people, exhorts them, and, in answer to their requests, promises to write a letter to the nine and a half tribes and another letter to the two and a half tribes of the exiles in Babylon. The book breaks off with the text of the letter to the nine and a half tribes.

Genre

Form-critically, the book resembles IV Ezra, to which it is also related in subject matter. Like IV Ezra, it consists of several genres: dialogues between the author and God or an angel, who speaks (cf. Zech. 1:9, etc.: המלאך הדבר בי) usually in prose, with occasional interruptions of poetry; prayers, usually exhibiting metrical structure, closely related to the Psalms but interwoven with reflective passages; exhortations; and vision narratives followed by interpretation. In other words, various genres have been combined. The themes also seem to have been of diverse origin. This variety accounts for many irregularities, whose presence led R. H. Charles to distinguish several sources differing in their eschatological hopes. But it seems more reasonable to assume that the author drew on a variety of materials and images than that we are dealing with a conglomerate of different sources.

Place and Date

There is a reasonable concensus among scholars that the book was written around A.D. 90; the author looks back on the destruction of the Temple and the city in the year 70, but knows nothing of the revolt under Bar Kochba. This argument does not rule out R. H. Charles' theory: he views the three apocalypses 27–30:1; 36–40; 53–74 as earlier sections, written before A.D. 70. It still remains a matter of debate, however, in view of the many points of contact between the Apocalypse of Baruch and IV Ezra, whether the former or the latter is earlier. At present, the scales are tipped in favor of an earlier origin for IV Ezra. It is reasonably certain that the book was composed in Jerusalem. The author has points of contact with the Pharisees.

Significance

The Syriac Apocalypse of Baruch is a book of comfort. Following the catastrophe of A.D. 70, and with muted polemic against Christianity, the author seeks to answer questions about the reward of the righteous and the punishment of the godless by looking ahead to the salvation that will come when the Messiah appears to inaugurate his kingdom and to the resurrection of the dead that will then take place.

D. From the Sphere of Influence of Qumran

Jubilees

Text: Ethiopic—A. Dillmann, *Liber Jubilaeorum, aethiopice,* 1859; R. H. Charles, *The Ethiopic Version of the Hebrew Book of Jubilees,* 1895. Latin—A. M. Ceriani, *Monumenta sacra et profana,* I/1 (1861):9–54, 63–64; H. Rönsch, *Das Buch der Jubiläen oder die Kleine Genesis,* 1874. Hebrew—*DJD,* III, plates, p. xv, text, 77–79.

Translations: Charles (R. H. Charles), II:1–82; Kautzsch (E. Littmann), II:31–119; Riessler, pp. 539–666; Kahana (M. Goldman), 2nd ed., 1956; Hammershaimb (B. Noack), 1958.

Monographs: R. North, *Sociology of the Biblical Jubilee,* 1954, pp. 70ff.; H. Cazelles and E. Vogt, "Sur les origines du calendrier des Jubilés," *Bib,* XLIII (1962):202–16; E. Kutsch, "Die Solstitien im Kalender des Jubiläenbuches und im äth. Henoch 72," *VT,* XII (1962):203–7; J. M. Baumgarten, "הלוח של ספר היובלים והמקרא," *Tarbits,* XXXIV/4 (1962/63):317–28; E. Hilgert, "The Jubilees Calendar and the Origin of Sunday Observance," *Andrews*

JUDAISM OUTSIDE THE HEBREW CANON

University Seminary Studies, I (1963):44–51; W. Baars and R. Zuurmond, "The Project for a New Edition of the Ethiopic Book of Jubilees," *JSS,* IX (1964):67–74; A. Rofe, "קטעים מכתב יר כוסף ס'היובלים במערה מסיל של קומראן," *Tarbits,* XXXIV/4 (1964/65):333–36; É. Cothenet, "Le Livre des Jubilés," *Catholicisme,* VI/25 (1965):1123–28; W. Wirgin, *The Book of Jubilees and the Maccabean Era of Smittah Circles,* Leeds University Oriental Society Monograph Series, Vol. 7, 1965; M. Baillet, "Remarques sur le manuscrit du livre des Jubilés de la grotte 3 de Qumran," *RQ,* V (1964/66):423–33; R. Deichgräber, "Fragmente einer Jubiläenhandschrift aus Höhle 3 von Qumran," *RQ,* V (1964/66):415–22; J. T. Milik, "Fragment d'une source du Psautier et Fragments des Jubilés, du Document de Damas, d'un phylactère dans la grotte 4 de Qumran," *RB,* LXXIII (1966):94–106, pl. i-iii.

BHH, II:897–98 (M. Weise); *RGG,* III:960–61 (L. Rost); Eissfeldt, pp. 821–24, 1023 (English: 606–8, 773); *IDB,* II:1002–3.

Text

The complete Book of Jubilees is extant in four Ethiopic manuscripts dating from the fifteenth through the nineteenth centuries; two are in Paris, one is in the British Museum, and one is in the library of the University of Tübingen. In 1859, A. Dillmann published the text of the book on the basis of two late manuscripts; in 1895 R. H. Charles published a new edition on the basis of the four known manuscripts. In 1861, A. M. Ceriani published fragments of a Latin translation comprising about a quarter of the text; these were republished in 1874 by H. Rönsch, with newly proposed emendations. Quotations from Epiphanius', *Peri métrōn kai stathmōn* bear witness to a Greek translation on which both the Ethiopic and Latin versions depend. Finally, fragments of no less than nine different Hebrew manuscripts of the work have been discovered at Qumran, evidence of the importance attached to the book there.

This means that the Book of Jubilees was originally composed in Hebrew, as Hebraisms in the translations also indicate; then about the beginning of the Christian era it was translated into Greek, probably in Hellenistic Egypt. According to Rönsch, the Latin translation was probably made from the Greek version during the fifth century C.E. The Ethiopic version also derives from the Greek.

Title

In the Ethiopic version, the work is entitled *maṣḥafa kufālē* in both superscription and colophon. Hebrew sources attest two titles, היובלים and בראשית זוטה, to which the Greek titles *Tà Iōbēlaĩa* or *Hoi Iōbēlaĩoi* and *Hē leptē Génesis* correspond. Other terms also appear in the literature of the early church, such as the Apocalypse or Testament of Moses, the Book of the Daughters of Adam, or the Life of Adam.

Contents

The book begins with God addressing Moses on the sixteenth day of the third month of the first year of the Exodus and commanding him to climb the mountain and receive the two stone tablets with the Law. Then, at God's command, the angel of the presence speaks and recounts the course of history from the moment of creation to Moses' receipt of the Law.

Style and Genre

The book purports to be the words of God spoken to Moses, followed by the narrative of the "angel of the presence." The latter recounts (with many corrections, expansions, and abbreviations) the primal history, the history of the patriarchs, and the events in Egypt as far as the giving of the Law to Moses upon an unnamed mountain. The narrator follows P more closely than the other Pentateuchal sources. Unlike P, however, he describes Adam as having already performed a sweet-smelling incense offering (3:27) and Noah as having performed a sin offering and a burnt offering (6:2-3). He traces a series of legal requirements back to the primal history; for example, the regulations governing the uncleanness of a woman after the birth of a son or daughter are associated with Adam and Eve in Paradise. Above all, he places the entire narrative within the framework of an absolute chronology based on weeks of years and Jubilee years, thus compensating for what he felt to be a deficiency on the part of P in Genesis.

We find a counterpart in the Genesis Apocryphon from Qumran (1QGenApoc), which paraphrases part of the primal history and the Abraham stories in midrashic fashion. But the interests of the authors are quite different. The legal material is much more extensive in the Book of Jubilees; it is treated with much greater importance and is incorporated more thoroughly into the narratives. The Genesis Apocryphon also has no absolute chronology.

Date

The date of composition can be determined with some precision. R. H. Charles points out that Levi (32:1) is called "priest of the Most High God," a title used only by the Hasmonean high priests. If the account of the destruction of Samaria (30:4-6) were interpreted as referring to the fate of Samaria when it was captured by Hyrcanus, we would be dealing with the last years of this particular Hasmonean and could follow Charles in proposing the period 109–105. There is nothing to contradict this hypothesis in the appearance of fragments at Qumran.

Author

A. Jellinek, in his *Bet ha-midrash* (1853–55), had already characterized the author as an Essene. This view must be accepted if the Qumran community is considered an Essene monastic community, as seems most likely. The author may actually have lived at Qumran and thus been a member of the inner circle, perhaps even of the group to which research into the Torah was entrusted. Such a suggestion cannot be demonstrated, although there is much evidence in its favor. In any case, the author lived in Palestine.

The Calendar

The unique aspect of the Book of Jubilees is its detailed calendar, constructed on the basis of a solar year comprising 364 days and equal quarters of 13 weeks. This calendar provides fixed dates for the festivals, of which the Feast of Weeks receives special emphasis, having been first celebrated by Noah after the Deluge. Abraham was the first man on earth to celebrate the Feast of Booths, on the day of Isaac's birth. Only Passover was too intimately associated with the exodus from Egypt to be traced back to an earlier age. But this calendar is also the calendar of the Qumran sect, which appears as well in the Damascus Document and in Enoch. There are many points of contact between Jubilees and the Damascus Document, including the general train of thought.

Significance

The Book of Jubilees is based on the Pentateuch, or at least Genesis and the first twenty chapters of Exodus. It presents a periphrastic revision of the narratives, deriving a wealth of legal regulations in the Torah from situations encountered in the primal history and the patriarchal period. The strictness of these regulations is in accord with the Essene ideal. It also shows how a member of the Qumran sect could interpret Genesis and Exodus in such a way as to confirm his own interpretation of the Law.

Ethiopic Enoch

Text: A. Dillmann, *Liber Henoch aethiopice,* 1851; J. Flemming, *Das Buch Henoch; äthiopischer Text,* 1902; R. H. Charles, *The Ethiopic Version of the Book of Enoch . . . Together with the Fragmentary Greek and Latin Versions,* 1906.

Greek—L. Radermacher, *Das Buch Henoch*, hrsg. . . . von J. Flemming und L. Radermacher, 1901, pp. 18–60, 113–14; Swete, III:789–808; *Pseudepigrapha Veteris Testamenti*, III (M. Black and A. M. Denis), 1968. Hebrew—Fragments in *DJD*, I, pp. 84–86, pl. xv.

Translations: Charles (R. H. Charles), II:163–281; Kautzsch (G. Beer), II:217–310; Riessler, pp. 355–451, 1291–97; Hammershaimb (E. Hammershaimb), 1956; Kahana (A. Kahana and J. Feitlowitz), 2nd ed., 1956.

Monographs: T. Klauser, "Der Vorhang vor dem Throne Gottes," *JbAC*, III (1960):141–42; E. Kutsch, "Die Solstitien im Kalender des Jubiläenbuches und im äth. Henoch 72," *VT*, XII (1962):205–7; A. Caquot and P. Geoltrain, "Notes sur le texte éthiopien des 'Paraboles' d'Henoch," *Sem*, XIII (1963):39–54; S. Agouridis, "Enōch," *Thresk EthEnkm* V (1964):706–8; G. Widengren, "Iran and Israel in Parthian Times with Special Regard to the Ethiopic Book of Enoch," *Temenos*, II (1966):139–77; G. Reese, "Die Geschichte Israels in der Auffassung des frühen Judentums," dissertation, Heidelberg, WS 1967/68.

BHH, II:692–93 (B. Reicke); *RGG*, III:222–25 (O. Plöger), Eissfeldt, pp. 836–43, 1024 (English: 617–22, 774).

Text

The Book of Enoch is preserved in its entirety only in Ethiopic. The earliest of the twenty-nine manuscripts used by R. H. Charles as the basis for his edition derives from the sixteenth century (R. H. Charles, pp. 165–66). The Ethiopic translation, which dates from around 500, was prepared on the basis of a Greek translation, two fragments of which (1:1–32:6 and 19:3–21:9) were discovered at Akhmîm by the Mission Archéologique Française in 1886/87 and published by M. Bouriant in 1892. Another Greek fragment is in the Vatican Library. The Greek translation goes back to a Semitic original. The debate over whether this original was written in Aramaic or in Hebrew has not been settled by discoveries at Qumran, where fragments of ten Aramaic manuscripts have been found, containing among other things Enoch 30:1–32:3; 35:1–36:4; and 77:3 and parts of the fifth book, including the Apocalypse of Ten Weeks, but not containing any trace of the Similitudes (chapters 37–71). R. H. Charles, however, considers it probable that these passages had a Hebrew original, while J. T. Milik ascribes them to a second-century revision and rearrangement, which could also favor a Hebrew text.

Following the model of the Pentateuch, the Psalter, and the Psalms of Solomon, the final author divided the Book of Enoch into five sections; since about the sixteenth century, this division has been replaced by a division into 108 chapters. The five sections are as follows: I, chapters 1–36; II, chapters 37–71; III, chapters 72–82; IV, chapters 83–90; and V, chapters 91–104. Chapters 105–108 constitute a conclusion. Division by subject matter reveals a different structure. Chapters 1–5 recount an introductory speech by Enoch describing the coming judgment of the world. Chapters 6–16 constitute angelology—the fall of the angels and the announcement of their punishment by Noah and again by Enoch. Chapters 17–19 and 20–36 are two accounts of Enoch's journeys through the earth, the heavens, and the underworld as well as explanations of meteorological and eschatological secrets. Chapters 37–71 contain messianology and an introduction (37). They also include discourses on the future dwelling place of the righteous and the ministry of the angels, together with astrological and meteorological information (38–44); discourses on the Messiah, who has been existing since before the Ancient of Days, and his judgment, and on the fount of righteousness, the resurrection, and the eschatological attack of the Gentiles upon Jerusalem (45–57); and details of the judgment of the Son of man upon men and angels (58–69) and Enoch's entrance into Paradise and his appointment as Son of man (70–71). Chapters 72–82 contain material on astronomy and the calendar; they deal with the course of the sun and moon, intercalary days, the stars, the compass and its cardinal points, the phases of the moon, and the rulers of each year (72–80; 82:4b-20). The conclusion of Enoch's journeys is found in chapters 81:1–82:4. Chapters 83–90 unfold a dream vision of the coming Deluge (83–84), as well as symbolic imagery depicting the course of history from Adam to the coming of the Messiah (85–90). Chapters 91–105 are exhortations addressed to Enoch's children, including in 93:1–14 and 91:12-17 the Apocalypse of Ten Weeks, which seeks to represent the entire course of history down to the age of salvation beginning with a universal judgment. Chapters 106–108 conclude the book, recounting the birth of Noah as accompanied by miracles and recording a final exhortation by Enoch.

It is easy to see from this survey that many strata of material are present. The book was put together in the course of a century out of traditions associated with the names of Noah and Enoch. In these traditions, both figures count as recipients and vehicles of a complex body of divine secrets. References to the marriages of the angels (Gen. 6:1-4) and to the prehistory of the Deluge attempt to explain portions of Scripture; accounts of the future down to the judgment and the age of salvation attempt to supplement and continue the prophetic and apocalyptic traditions of the Old Testament; other passages, finally, seek to explain cosmic mysteries such as the movements of the sun, moon, and stars. We may assume that these traditions, deriving from many sources, including the surrounding world of the ancient Near East, frequently circulated independently. Coherent units like the complex of Noah traditions, the short Apocalypse of Ten Weeks, and the Treatise on Astronomy probably existed independently until they finally were incorporated with new exhortations, speculations, symbolic narratives, etc., into the present Book of Enoch.

Title

The manuscripts do not give any title to Ethiopic Enoch, also called I Enoch. The early church cites it as Enoch, the Book of Enoch, or the Words of Enoch.

The Growth of the Book of Enoch

As noted above, a Book of Noah has been included with the Enoch traditions; we shall deal with it first. It is found in 6–11; 39:1-2a; 54:7–55:2; 60; 65:1–69:25; and 106–107, albeit in incomplete and fragmentary form. The beginning, which would introduce the figure of Noah to speak what follows, has been lost. The interpolation of this book took place very early. For example, the list of fallen angels designates Azazel as their leader in chapter 8; chapter 6 records Semyaza in the same role. The most important themes are: the fall of the angels and the details of the angels' pernicious secret arts made known to men at the time of their fall; the threatened Deluge and the vision of a paradisal age of salvation without any messianic figure; and an account of the birth of Noah as being accompanied by miracles. The Book of Noah is mentioned in Jubilees 10:13 and 21:10. It is less likely that these Noah fragments derive from a Book of Lamech, mentioned in a Greek list of apocryphal writings, than from Enoch. The Book of Noah presupposes the existence of an Enoch tradition. It probably came into being in Palestine (specifically, Jerusalem) around the beginning of the second century B.C. before the appearance of the Maccabees.

The Apocalypse of Ten Weeks in chapters 93 and 91:12-17 is at least as early as the Book of Noah and possibly even earlier. It may originally have been limited to seven weeks and later expanded. J. P. Thornton has suggested that it is a secret history of the Qumran sect. If so, the conclusion, at least, would be somewhat later. The commonly accepted view, however, finds no mention of the Maccabean period; rather, it concludes that the number of apostates implies that only certain righteous individuals are elected to enjoy the age of salvation that follows directly.

This theory would date the Apocalypse of Ten Weeks prior to the Maccabean period, in other words around 170 B.C. The Apocalypse of the Animals (85–90) contains an account of history from Adam to the Hasmoneans and concludes with a vision of the messianic age. The figures belonging to the primal history, like the figure of the Messiah, are symbolized by bulls; the figures of the patriarchs and their descendants down to the Hasmonean period are represented by sheep; their opponents are symbolized by wolves and other wild beasts. The section is the second earliest. Depending on whether it concludes with Judas Maccabeus or ends with John Hyrcanus or even Alexander Jannaeus, it belongs to the middle or end of the second century, or to the first quarter of the first century B.C.

Chapters 12–16 provide more details about Enoch's role of mediator in the punishment of the fallen angels. Since they constitute an expansion and correction of the corresponding material from the Book of Noah, they must have come later, but they probably still date from the first half of the second century B.C.

Chapters 17–19 and 20–36 contain the first and second journeys of Enoch through the various regions of the earth, the heavens, and the underworld, with special emphasis on the dwelling places of the blessed and the places where sinners and fallen angels are punished. These chapters probably belong to the second century B.C. also.

Chapters 37–71, following an introduction in chapter 37, comprise three discourses made up of similitudes or parables (38–44; 45–47; and 58–69), together with appendices and supplements, into which the fragments of the Book of Noah mentioned above have been incorporated. The similitudes furnish information about the hierarchy of the angels and reveal atmospheric, meteorological, and astronomical secrets; they culminate in the appointment of Enoch as the Son of man. They contain various traditions dating from earlier ages but in their present recension cannot be designated earlier than the first century B.C. J. T.

Milik dates them as late as the second century C.E., above all because there is no trace of them at Qumran.

Chapters 72–82 constitute an astronomical treatise, probably written around the end of the second century B.C. Chapters 94–105 contain exhortations of Enoch in the style of the farewell discourses of the twelve patriarchs. These discourses date from the first century B.C. The beginning of the book (chapters 1–5) and the conclusion (chapter 108) are among the redactional additions to this complex book. They date from the first century B.C. Nothing in the book makes any allusion to the coming of the Romans in 63 B.C.

We may conclude—if we disregard the suggestion of J. T. Milik mentioned above—that the individual sections of the book came into being during the second and first centuries B.C., while the final redaction can be assigned to the end of this period. If Milik's thesis is accepted, the book gradually came into being over the course of four hundred years and was not finished until the second century C.E.

Place

Jerusalem was probably the place where the individual sections were composed and the present book was assembled. The evidence of the Qumran fragments suggests that the original language was Aramaic, with the possible exception of chapters 37–71, which could have been in Hebrew. The group responsible for the book's composition exhibits marked similarities to the Qumran sect (calendar, angelology), but cannot be identified exactly with it. There is no trace, for instance, of the dualism of the Manual of Discipline (1QS) or the notion of two messianic figures, one out of Aaron and one out of Israel. The Book of Enoch proves to be an important collection of revelations ascribed to Enoch, explaining obscure Old Testament passages, especially the events in the angelic realm that inform Genesis 6:1-5, as well as natural phenomena such as could still evoke awe from Job. Early Christianity, too, as late as the period of the New Testament Canon (Jude), considered the book a divine revelation. Not until the sixth century was it suppressed within the sphere of Mediterranean Christendom, while still holding a place of respect in the Ethiopic Church.

Significance

The Book of Enoch is a collection of attempts to solve riddles of Scripture, of nature, and of the world and its extraterrestrial history both primeval and eschatological—for example—the fall of the angels, the fate of the righteous and the godless in a world to come, the secret of the Messiah, the annual cycle of sunrise and sunset, etc. It is closely related to the milieu of Qumran, without being identical. The editor stands in the service of a group who brooded over problems of theology and the cosmos, trying to provide its members with solutions and to give them courage to attain a life of eternal bliss by way of righteous conduct according to the commandments of the Torah.

Testaments of the Twelve Patriarchs

Text: Greek—R. H. Charles, *The Greek Versions of the Testaments of the Twelve Patriarchs*, 1908, reprinted 1960; M. de Jonge, *Testamenta XII Patriarcharum*. Armenian—S. Josepheantz, *Schatz alter und neuer Väter; I. Nichtkanonische Schriften des AT*, 1896. Slavonic—N. Tichonravov, *Pamiatniki otretčennoi russkoi literaturii*, I, 1863, pp. 96–232. Aramaic—fragments in *DJD*, I, pp. 87–91, pl. xvii. Hebrew—Cambridge texts published by H. L. Passand and J. Arendzen in *JQR*, XII (1899/1900):651–61; Oxford texts published by R. H. Charles and A. Cowley in *JQR*, XIX (1906/1907):566–83.

Translations: Charles (R. H. Charles), II:282–367; Kautzsch (F. Schnapp), II:458–88, 492–506, and (E. Kautzsch) II:489–92 (Test. Naphtali from the Chronicles of Jerahmeel); Riessler, pp. 1149–1250, 1335–38; Kahana (I. Ostersetzer), 2nd ed., 1956.

Monographs: M. W. C. de Jonge, "Once More: Christian Influence in the Testaments of the Patriarchs," *NT*, V (1962):311–19; G. Widengren, "Royal Ideology and the Testaments of the Twelve Patriarchs," in *Festschrift S. E. Hooke*, 1963, pp. 202–12; B. Murmelstein, "Das Lamm in Test. Jos. 19,8," *ZNW*, LVIII (1967):273–79; J. Becker, *Untersuchungen zur Entstehungsgeschichte der Testamente der Zwölf Patriarchen*, 1969; M. E. Stone, *The Testament of Levi; a First Study of the Armenian Mss. of the Testaments of the XII Patriarchs in the Convent of St. James*, 1969.

BHH, III:1955 (M. Philonenko); *RGG*, VI:701–702 (L. Rost); Eissfeldt, pp. 855–62, 1024 (English: 631–36, 775); *IDB*, IV:575–79.

Text

The Testaments are preserved in nine Greek manuscripts dating from the tenth to the seventeenth century; in some they are independent, in others they constitute an appendix to the Septuagint. These manuscripts are found at Oxford, Cambridge, Rome, Mount Athos, Paris, Patmos, and Sinai. There are also two later seventeenth-century copies of the Cambridge manuscript, with some omissions. The work is also extant in twelve Armenian manuscripts dating from the thirteenth to the seventeenth century, found in Venice, London, Etshmiadzin, Rome, Oxford, and Vienna. These represent two recensions. There are also two Slavonic translations. All these translations are based on a Hebrew original that must likewise have been extant in two recensions, since only this explanation can account for several variants in the two Greek recensions that derive from errors in translation. To date, fragments of Aramaic manuscripts of the Testament of Levi have been found in Caves 1 and 4 at Qumran, some of which are closely related to an Aramaic fragment of the same Testament from the Cairo Genizah. The Genizah fragment, however, contains a longer text—like that attested in the Greek manuscript from Mount Athos. Other fragments from Cave 4, however, agree with the standard text. In addition, a Hebrew fragment of the Testament of Naphtali has come to light in Cave 4.

These discoveries complicate the history of the text. One hypothesis might run as follows: Originally there was only an Aramaic Testament of Levi, in the longer recension, to which was added—for what reason?—a Hebrew Testament of Naphtali. Then a shorter Hebrew recension of the Testament of Levi came into existence alongside the Testament of Naphtali. Later—after the destruction of Qumran?—these were added to the series of the Testaments of the Twelve Patriarchs, perhaps due to Christian influence, since traces of Christian ideas can be found at least in the interpolations. Such an explanation is possible, but we shall probably have to wait until all the Qumran fragments have been edited before we can come any closer to the real solution.

Title

The Greek title varies. Alongside *Diathēkai tōn dōdeka patriarchōn tōn huiōn Iakōb* we also find *Hai Diathēkai tōn ib' patriarchōn pròs toùs huioùs autōn* and, briefly, *Patriárchai.* The individual Testaments probably were originally titled *Diathēkē Roubēn huioū Israēl,* and so on.

Contents

The twelve Testaments are farewell discourses of the patriarchs delivered just before their deaths and based on certain events in their lives—usually events associated with Joseph. They conclude with admonitions, each attacking a certain vice of which a patriarch was guilty or from which, thanks to the help of Yahweh, he escaped. The individual testaments run as follows:

Reuben takes as his point of departure the outrage recorded in Genesis 35:22 and 49:4 and goes on to speak of the seven spirits given each man by Beliar. He finds these spirits of Beliar at work whenever a man gazes at a woman or lies with her. Finally, Reuben counsels obedience to Levi.

Simon charges himself with having been angry at Judah for selling Joseph instead of killing him and in his admonition, cautions against envy. He concludes with a vision of the age of salvation, when two messiahs will appear, one out of Levi and another out of Judah.

Levi takes as his point of departure the revenge that he and Simeon took upon Hamor (Gen. 34:25) and then recounts two dreams. The first takes him on a journey through the seven heavens, while the second describes his investiture as a priest by men in white raiment. He cautions against pride, demands respect for the priesthood, and concludes with a vision of the priest-messiah.

Judah speaks of his deeds as a herdsman and warrior, as well as of the events recounted in Genesis 38. Then he warns against wine, admonishes his hearers to love Levi, and closes with a vision of the age of salvation.

Issachar recalls Genesis 30:14ff. and praises his simple way of life, which he recommends to his descendants.

Zebulun tells of the pity he had for Joseph, which prevented him from taking part in the outrage committed by his brothers, exhorts his hearers to show mercy and pity, and looks forward to the final appearance of the Lord.

Dan confesses that he rejoiced over the sale of Joseph and warns against falsehood and anger. He, too, looks forward to leaders coming out of Judah and Levi in the age of salvation.

Naphtali boasts of his descent from Bella, the handmaiden of Rachel, extols Yahweh as the God of order, and recounts two dreams that justify the preeminence of Levi and Judah and the ambition of Joseph. He concludes with an exhortation to good conduct.

Gad tells how he hated Joseph, then cautions against hate, and demands patience to await God's judgment.

Asher does not cite any incident; in his exhortations he speaks of the two ways that God has placed before men.

Joseph recounts the crafty temptations of the Egyptian

woman and boasts of his chastity, which he inculcates in his children.

Benjamin speaks of the death of his mother when she gave birth to him, then tells of a conversation with Joseph in Egypt, and, finally, exhorts his hearers to purity of mind.

This survey shows that the Testaments of Levi and Naphtali depart somewhat from the norm in stressing dreams as prefigurations of future events. The Testament of Joseph, as well, differs in structure from the majority of the Testaments, in that the stories of the temptations of the Egyptian woman run through the entire work; the exhortation is totally interwoven with the narrative and does not constitute an independent section of the Testament. These departures from the regular pattern of the Testaments, as well as the Christian interpolations that appear in almost every Testament, suggest that they underwent a lengthy period of development.

Origin

The date and milieu proper to the Testaments has been a matter of debate ever since the manuscripts were discovered. Most recently M. de Jonge has attempted to demonstrate that they were composed by a Christian author around A.D. 200 on the basis of earlier Jewish traditions. The author, according to de Jonge, had only the Testaments of Levi and Naphtali before him; the rest of his material he drew from the traditions of the Book of Jubilees and the midrashim in order to preach his Christian ethics using the sons of Jacob as examples. Similar theories are espoused by J. T. Milik and E. F. Sutcliffe.

A contrary hypothesis is supported by A. Dupont-Sommer, who sees the Testaments originating around 100 B.C. within the Qumran community, arguing on the grounds that the Damascus Document quotes a series of testaments. It would be more accurate to say that the Damascus Document and the Testaments draw on the same tradition; Dupont-Sommer is right in assigning the Testaments to the same stream of tradition as the Damascus Document. Further evidence for this view is provided by the Aramaic fragments of the Testament of Levi from Caves 1 and 4 at Qumran and the Hebrew fragment of the Testament of Naphtali likewise found at Qumran. But the process is more complex, as the existence side by side of Aramaic fragments of the Testament of Levi and a Hebrew fragment of the Testament of Naphtali show. It was pointed out above that these two Testaments belong to a different genre than the others. They are unique in focusing on two dreams that prefigure the future. The Testament of Levi is probably the earlier of the two; it goes back to the early Maccabean period and may be intended to justify Jonathan's assumption of the office of high priest in 153 B.C. Later, when the hegemony of the Maccabees came to extend further to the north, the Hebrew Testament of Naphtali was added, which alluded to the history of the divided kingdom in two dreams and, from the perspective of late Judaism, warned against union with the Samaritans. Furthermore, Tobit was also a member of the Naphtali tribe, and Ahikar also sought to associate this book with this tribe. Only afterwards did the other Testaments come into existence—perhaps not until the first century C.E.—while a final Christian redaction can be dated around 200.

The Testaments were written in Palestine, the earliest at Qumran, the later ones in circles closely connected with Qumran.

Significance

The Testaments of Levi and Naphtali illustrate the high esteem late Judaism had for the interpretation of dreams and the strength with which men believed that dreams could help foretell future events; the exact repetition of a dream bore witness to the importance and truth of the vision it contained. For the rest, the Testaments contain moral exhortations touched by the spirit of the Qumran community but free from many of its peculiar features (for example, strict observance of the Law, bravado over possession of the correct liturgical calendar, and high esteem for ritual ablutions). The exhortations were obviously not meant for the inner circle of observants, but for the more extended circle of devotees and proselytes. This explains why the early church gladly appropriated them with only minimal revision—all the more so because they appeared to seek rapprochement with the popular philosophy of Hellenism. Their appeal to (Slavonic) Enoch gained them further respect.

Assumption of Moses

Text: Latin—A. M. Ceriani, *Monumenta sacra et profana*, I/1, 1861, 9–13; C. Clemen, *Die Himmelfahrt des Mose*, KIT, 10, 1904. Retranslation into Greek—A. Hilgenfeld, *Messias Judaeorum*, 1869, pp. 435–68.

Translations: Charles (R. Charles), II:407–24; Kautzsch (C. Clemen), II:311–31; Riessler, pp. 485–95, 1301–1303; Kahana (A. Kahana), 2nd ed., 1956.

Monographs: J. Licht, "Taxo, or the Apocalyptic Doctrine of Vengeance," *JSSt*, XII (1961):95–103.

BHH, II:1243–44 (D. H. Wallace); *RGG*, III:337 (R. Meyer); Eissfeldt, pp. 844–46 (English: 623–24); *IDB*, III:450–51 (M. Rist).

Text

The Ambrosian Library in Milan preserves a sixth-century palimpsest of eight folio pages, with writing on both sides, which contains a Latin translation of a Greek version of the Assumption of Moses, which in turn goes back to an original that was more likely Hebrew than Aramaic. Neither the original nor the Greek translation has survived. Quotations in the Epistle of Jude and the Church Fathers may have been taken from the Greek translation. Ecclesiastical writers use various titles to refer to extracanonical Moses documents, e.g., a "Testament of Moses" *(Diathēke Mōuséōs)* and an "Ascension" or "Assumption of Moses" *(Análēpsis Mōuséōs)*.

Title

The first three lines, possibly written in red, have faded completely. They probably contained the title—which may have been "Prophecy of Moses" *(Prophēteia Mōuséōs;* C. Clemen) or "Testament of Moses" *(Diathēkē Mōuséōs;* R. H. Charles and others). The work is usually called the "Assumption (or 'Ascension') of Moses" *(Análēpsis Mōuséōs),* on the theory that the legend of Moses' assumption was added as a second section, though no longer preserved. The Epistle of Jude presupposes such a legend.

Contents

At the age of 120, Moses prophesies before the ears of Joshua, whom he finally appoints to be his successor. Although the world was, he says, created for the sake of the Law, to prevent the Law from being revealed to all mankind, Moses had already been set apart even before the beginning of the world to make it known to the Israelites alone. Moses instructs Joshua to conceal the Scriptures. He himself is to lead the people into the promised land. The following section recounts the history of Israel and the Jews down to the time of Herod and his sons after the manner of Daniel 10–12, which ultimately goes back to Gen. 15:13-16. Now, at the height of oppression and moral depravity, appears Taxo, of the tribe of Levi, who with his seven sons would rather suffer death than transgress the Law. He hopes by means of this sacrifice to bring about the coming of the Lord of Lords and other cosmic apocalyptic events, thus precipitating God's judgment upon sinners and salvation for the righteous. Moses himself wishes to rest and let Joshua take over leadership of the people. Joshua protests and declares that if the tomb of Moses were to be in keeping with Moses' greatness, it would have to extend over the whole earth. He could not possibly be the successor to such a powerful man. Moses, however, sets the hesitant Joshua right by referring to God's predestination. At this point, the manuscript breaks off. If the quotations in the Epistle of Jude and in the Church Fathers belong to this work (as C. Clemen assumes with respect to most of them), there followed the death of Moses, the appearance of the archangel Michael, Michael's struggle with Satan for the body of Moses, and finally a scene like that involving Michael in the Life of Adam and Eve. The fragmentary nature of the manuscript leaves room for this and other hypotheses.

Author, Place, and Date

As early as 1868, M. Schmidt and A. Merx described the author as an Essene, but they were unable to gain acceptance of their hypothesis. The discovery of the Qumran manuscripts proved them correct to the extent of confirming that the author belonged to the Qumran milieu (R. Meyer, O. Eissfeldt). There are particularly close connections with the Damascus Document and the War Scroll. The association with Qumran means that the work was composed in Palestine. Since the Temple appears to be still standing, whereas Herod is dead and his sons appear to be ruling, the date must fall in the first third of the first century C.E.

Significance

If the work came into being in association with the Qumran sect, we are dealing with an example of a genre especially popular there, as the Book of Jubilees and the Genesis Apocryphon show. The esteem enjoyed by the Mosaic Torah in these circles easily explains how legends about Moses going beyond what is recorded in the Torah could come into being and achieve written form.

The foreknowledge and providence of God, emphasized to the point of determinism, took on concrete form in the

148

person and prophecy of Moses. The attacks on the priests and Pharisees, almost reminiscent of those in the New Testament (Jesus), go beyond the statements of the Damascus Document, the Habakkuk Commentary, and the Nahum Commentary in revealing the gravamina of the Qumran sect and thus illuminate the religious situation preceding the public appearance of Jesus. Of particular interest in this regard is the eschatological vision with which the fragment closes.

Martyrdom of Isaiah

Text: A. Dillmann, *Ascensio Isaiae aethiopice et latine,* 1877; R. H. Charles, *The Ascension of Isaiah,* 1900; E. Tisserant, *L'Ascension d'Isaie,* 1909.

Translations: Charles (R. H. Charles), II:155–62; Kautzsch (G. Beer), II:119–27; Riessler, pp. 481–84, 1300–1301; G. H. Box, *The Apocalypse of Abraham and the Ascension of Isaiah,* 1919; W. Flemming and H. Duensing, "Die Himmelfahrt des Jesaja," in Hennecke, *Neutestamentliche Apokryphen,* II, 3rd ed., 1964, pp. 454–68; Hammbershaimb (E. Hammershaimb), 1959.

Monographs: K. Heussi, "Die Ascensio Isaiae und ihr vermeintliches Zeugnis für ein römisches Martyrium des Apostels Petrus," *WZJena,* XII (1963):269–74; A. Vaillant, "Un apocryphe pseudo-bogomile; la Vision d'Isaie," *RÈ-Slav,* XLII (1963):109–21; É. Cothenet, "L'Ascension de Isaie," Catholicisme, VI/23 (1963):144–46; M. Erbetta, "Ascensione di Isaia 4,3 è la testimonianza più antica del martirio di Pietro," *Euntes docete,* XIX (1966):427–36; M. Philonenko, "Le Martyre de Ésaie et l'histoire de la secte de Qoumrân," *CahRHPhR,* XLI (1967):1–25.

BHH, II:857 (B. Reicke); *RGG,* III:336–37 (R. Meyer); Eissfeldt, pp. 825–26 (English: 609–10); *IDB,* II:744–46 (M. Rist).

Text

The three short works brought together under this title, all focusing on the person of the prophet Isaiah, have been

149

preserved completely in the Ethiopic translation. It was made some time after the fifth century on the basis of a Greek text. Individual sections have also been preserved in Greek, Latin, Coptic, and Old Church Slavonic. We are interested here in the first section, which recounts the martyrdom of Isaiah. It was originally composed in Hebrew, but the original text has been lost. The other two sections, a vision of Isaiah and the ascension of Isaiah, are the work of Christian authors.

Title

Origen, in his commentary on Matthew 13:57, refers to the work as *Apókryphon Hēsaïou;* Jerome, in his commentary on Isaiah 44:4, speaks of it as *Ascensio Isaiae.* We also find the title *Horasis Hēsaïou,* and Cedrenus i. 102 refers to the work as *Diathēkē Hezekíou.* Riessler speaks of the Ascension of Isaiah but translated only the Martyrdom of Isaiah; Fohrer combines the two expressions into Martyrdom and Ascension of Isaiah. The term "Martyrdom of Isaiah" is usually taken as an adequate title for the Jewish portion of the work, especially because the Ascension is only mentioned in one of the Christian appendices.

Content

In 1:1-2a, 6b-13a; 2:1–3:12; and 5:1b-14 we read how Hezekiah, admonishing his son Manasseh in the presence of the prophet Isaiah, was interrupted by Isaiah, who predicted both the future sins of Manasseh and his own martyrdom at Manasseh's hands. The death of Hezekiah brings Manasseh to the throne. The latter, however, submits to Beliar, who tempts him into apostasy from Yahweh. Confronted with Manasseh's worship of Satan, Isaiah first withdraws to Bethlehem and finally into the desert of Judah, where he is surrounded by Micah, Hananiah, Joel, Habakkuk, and Shear-Jashub, wearing garments made of skins and living off the desert plants they gathered. Belchira betrays the hiding place of Isaiah, brings charges against him before Manasseh—citing some of his words out of context—and thus succeeds in having the prophet condemned to death. Isaiah meets death by being sawed in two.

Author, Place, and Date

The author was a Palestinian Jew. Since he considers that the marks of a true prophet of Yahweh include not only hairy clothing—cf. Elisha—but also the lifestyle of an anchorite and the use of wild plants exclusively for nourishment, he may well have been an Essene or at least someone closely related to the Essene movement. Thus a connection with Qumran is possible. In this case, the work may have been written as early as the second century B.C., perhaps under the influence of the oppressive rule of Antiochus Epiphanes. So far no trace of it seems to have been found at Qumran. On the other hand, Hebrews 11:37 appears to allude to it.

Significance

The legend, which may be dependent on Iranian legends (the three-headed serpent Azhi Dahaka slays Yima by sawing in two a tree in which the latter had taken refuge) belongs with the series of martyr legends from the Maccabean period—for example—the story of the three young men in the furnace, Daniel in the lion pit, or the seven brothers in IV Maccabees. Its purpose is to show that not even prophets like Isaiah escaped false accusations and eventual martyrdom, yet they remained true to Yahweh despite all their torments.

Life of Adam and Eve

Text: Latin—W. Meyer, "Vita Adae et Evae," *AAM*, XIV/3 (1878):185–250. Greek—C. von Tischendorf, "Apocalypsis Mosis," in *Apocalypses apocryphae*, 1866, pp. x–xii, 1–23; A. M. Ceriani, *Monumenta sacra et profana*, V/1 (1868):19–24.

Translations: Charles (L. S. A. Wells), II:123–54; Kautzsch (C. Fuchs), II:506–28; Riessler, pp. 668–81, 1311–12; Kahana (M. Haak), 2nd ed., 1956.

Monographs: E. C. Quinn, *The Quest of Seth for the Oil of Life*, 1962; *idem*, "The Quest of Seth, Solomon's Ship and the Grail," *Tradition*, XXI (1965):185–222; C. Sirat, "Un midraš en habit musulman: la vision de Moise sur le mont Sinai (aṭ-Tabari, Tafsīr ad Suram VII, 139–42)," *RHR*, CLXVIII (1965):15–28.

BHH, I:25 (H. Ringgren); *RGG*, I:91 (R. Meyer); Eissfeldt, 862–64 (English: 636–37); *IDB*, I:44–45 (B. J. Bamberger).

Text

There are two Jewish recensions of the Life of Adam and Eve; for the most part they parallel each other and probably represent different elaborations of a common original most likely written in Hebrew. No trace of such an original has been found, however. The Latin translation of the Life of Adam and Eve is preserved in many medieval manuscripts, which are divided by W. Meyer into four classes. The Apocalypse of Moses, which generally parallels the Life of Adam and Eve, has been preserved in Greek. Six manuscripts (located in Milan, Montpellier, Paris, Venice, and Vienna) are known; the earliest of them dates from the first century C.E. An Armenian translation and two Old Church Slavonic translations (one shorter than the other) exhibit marked Christian editorial revision. There are also purely Christian versions of the same material in Syriac, Arabic, and Coptic.

Title

The Latin title of the first group is *Vita Adae et Evae*, "Life of Adam and Eve." Tischendorf referred to the second as *Apocalypsis Mosis*, since all the manuscripts state that the book was imparted to Moses through the archangel Michael.

Contents

Both traditions recount the fate of Adam and Eve following their banishment from Paradise, briefly mentioning Cain and Abel as well as the birth of Seth. Then they skip to Adam's mortal sickness, speak of the unsuccessful attempt on the part of Eve and Seth to beg the oil of Paradise that will heal the sick man, and describe (as a binding model for the future) the burial rites performed for Adam by the angels under the direction of the archangel Michael. Eight days later Eve dies and is likewise buried by angels.

Now to the differences between the two traditions. The Life of Adam and Eve begins by describing the plight of the two exiles and their fruitless search for food now that they no longer have the food of Paradise and find themselves forced to eat what the animals eat. Adam and Eve thereupon decide to do penance—Adam for forty days, Eve for thirty-seven. Eve will stand in the Tigris in water to her neck; Adam will do the same in the Jordan (possibly a substitute for the Gihon, a river in Paradise). Satan tempts Eve into ending her penance prematurely; Adam deplores her surrender to temptation and rebukes Satan, who defends himself by saying that it was on Adam's account that he was banished from the presence of God and sent to earth; thus his wrath, hatred, and envy toward Adam are justified. There follows the story of the birth of Cain and Abel, with which the Apocalypse of Moses begins.

Following the birth of Seth, the Life of Adam and Eve inserts another unique section, a vision in which Adam is promised that although he will die, God will hold a final judgment in the distant future that will end with the deliverance of the righteous and the perdition of sinners.

The story of Adam's illness at the age of 930 (he does not live out the thousand years that constitute a day of God) appears in roughly the same form in both traditions. Following this story, the Apocalypse of Moses inserts a highly embellished account of the role played by Eve in the fall and banishment from Paradise. At this juncture the two traditions once more run parallel in the account of the death and burial of Adam and Eve, although the Apocalypse contains a more expanded version.

Literary Problems

The variation in the way the material is handled probably antedates the Latin and Greek recensions. But it is no longer possible to determine the actual nature of the two texts before their translation nor the nature of the common original. In the Life of Adam and Eve, chapter 43:2-5 is a late Christian interpolation looking forward to the coming of Christ and then his descent into Hell to save Adam.

Author, Place, and Date

There can be no doubt that the lost original can be ascribed to a Jewish author who probably lived in Palestine—possibly toward the end of the first century B.C. The year A.D. 70 is the *terminus ante quem*, since the Temple—of Herod?—is still standing. The author may have had affinities with Essene circles, as the ascetic features (especially the Apocalypse's description of the physical separation of the sexes, even for animals) suggest.

Significance

The Adam stories seek to supplement the biblical account with edifying material. They show that serious repentance helps overcome the temptations man is subjected to by Satan, whose fall is associated with the creation of Adam. At the same time, however, they represent woman as more subject to temptation. The simple burial rites laid down by the archangel Michael and carried out by the angels may correspond to Essene customs observed at the burial site of Qumran.

The books of Adam represent a popular genre, as demonstrated also by the Genesis Apocryphon and the Book of Jubilees, as well as the Book of Noah incorporated into the Book of Enoch.

E. Qumran Manuscripts

Texts: M. Burrows, with the assistance of J. C. Trever and W. H. Brownlee, *The Dead Sea Scrolls of St. Mark's Monastery, I: The Isaiah Manuscript and the Habakkuk Commentary,* 1950; *idem, The Dead Sea Scrolls . . . , II/2: Plates and Transcription of the Manual of Discipline,* 1951; J.-D. Barthélemy and J. T. Milik (with contributions by R. de Vaux, G. M. Crowfoot, H. J. Plenderleith, and G. L. Harding), *Qumran Cave I* (*Discoveries in the Judaean Desert,* I), 1955; P. Benoit, J. T. Milik, and R. de Vaux, *Les Grottes de Murabba 'at* (*Discoveries in the Judaean Desert,* II), 1960; M. Baillet, J. T. Milik, and R. de Vaux, *Les 'Petites Grottes' de Qumran* (*Discoveries in the Judaean Desert of Jordan,* III), 1962; J. A. Sanders, *The Psalms Scroll of Qumran Cave 11 (11QPs*[a]*)* (*Discoveries in the Judaean Desert,* IV), 1965; J. M. Allegro, with the collaboration of A. A. Anderson, *Qumrân Cave 4 I (4Q 158–4Q 186)* (*Discoveries in the Judaean Desert,* V), 1968; E. L. Sukenik, מגילות גנוזות מתוך גנזה קדומה שנמצאה במדבר יהודה I, 1948; II, 1950; *idem,* אוצר המגילות הגנוזות שבידי האוניברסיטה העברית, 1955; with English text: *The Dead Sea Scrolls of the Hebrew University,* 1955. N. Avigad and Y. Yadin, *A Genesis Apocryphon from the Wilderness of Judaea,* 1956.

Translations: H. Bardtke, *Die Handschriftenfunde am Toten Meer,* I, 1952, 2nd ed. 1953; *idem, Die Handschriftenfunde am Toten Meer,* II, 1958, 2nd ed. 1961; M. Burrows, *The Dead Sea Scrolls with Translation,* 1956; *idem, More Light on the Dead Sea Scrolls,* 1958; J. Maier, *Die Texte vom Toten Meer,* I–II, 1960; J. Carmignac and P. Guilbert, *Les textes de Qumrân traduits et annotés,* II, 1963; K. G. Kuhn, *Konkordanz zu den Qumrantexten,* 1960; *idem,* with U. Müller, W. Schmücker, and H. Stegemann, "Nachträge zur Konkordanz su den Qumrantexten," *RQ,* IV (1962/63):277–78; F. Michelini-Tocci, *I Manoscritti de Mar Morto,* 1967; I. Matsuda, *Shikai bunsho,* 1963.

Discovery: W. H. Brownlee, "Muhammed ed-deeb's Own Story of His Scroll Discoveries," *JNESt,* XVI (1957):236–39, pl. xxxvi; J. C. Trever, "When was Qumran

Cave I Discovered?" *RQ,* III (1961/62):135–41; W. H. Brownlee, "Some New Facts Concerning the Discovery of the Scrolls of lQ," *RQ,* IV (1963/64):417–20.

Settlement: R. de Vaux, "Fouille au Khirbet Qumran," *RB,* LX (1953):83–106, pl. ii–vii; S. Schulz, "Chirbet ḳumrān, 'ēn feschcha und die buḳē'a," *ZDPV,* LXXVI (1960):50–72; L. M. Pákozdy, "Der wirtschaftliche Hintergrund der Gemeinschaft von Qumran," *LeipzSymp,* 1963, pp. 269–91; R. G. Boling, "Twenty Years of Discovery," *McCormick Quarterly,* XXI (1967/68):265–72; S. H. Steckoll, "Preliminary Excavation Report on the Qumran Cemetery," *RQ,* VI (1967/68):323–44; N. Haas and H. Nathan, "Anthropological Survey of the Human Skeletal Remains from Qumran," *RQ,* VI (1967/68):345–52.

Bibliography: C. Burchard, *Bibliographie zu den Handschriften vom Toten Meer,* BZAW, 76, 1957; II, BZAW, 89, 1965; J. van der Ploeg, "Les manuscrits du Désert de Juda; publications récentes importantes," *BiOr,* XXII (1965):133–42; M. Yizhar, *Bibliography of Hebrew Publications on the Dead Sea Scrolls 1948–1964,* Harvard Theological Studies 23, 1967; J. Carmignac, "Bibliographie," *RQ,* VI (1967/68):457–79; W. Tyloch, "Rekopisy znad Morza Martwego po dwudziestu latach," *Euhemer, Przeglad religioznawczy,* XII (1968), no. 2 (68), 21–38; Z. J. Kapera, "Polska bibliografia rekopisów znad Morza Martwego," *Euhemer, Przeglad religioznawczy,* XII (1968) no. 2 (68), 129–40.

Dating: F. M. Cross, Jr., "The Early History of the Qumran Community," *McCormick Quarterly,* XXI (1967/68):249–64; H. H. Rowley, "L'histoire de la secte Qumranienne," *BEThL,* XXIV/1 (De Mari à Qumran) (1967):272–301; S. Zeitlin, "The Expression 'betalmud' in the Scrolls Militates Against the Views of the Protagonists of Their Antiquity," *JQR,* NS LIV (1963/64):89–99; N. Drazin, "What Can 'betalmud' Prove?" *JQR,* NS LIV (1963/64):333; S. B. Hoenig, "The Pesher Nahum 'Talmud'," *JBL,* LXXXVI (1967):441–45; H. Haag, *Die Handschriftenfunde in der Wüste Juda,* 1965; C. Rabin and Y.

Yadin, *Aspects of the Dead Sea Scrolls,* 2nd ed., 1965; K. H. Rengstorf, *Hirbet Qumrân and the Problem of the Library of the DS Cave,* 1963; F. M. Cross, *The Ancient Library of Qumran and Modern Biblical Studies,* 1963; G. R. Driver, *The Judaean Scrolls; the Problem and a Solution,* 1965; C. Roth, "Qumran et Masadah; a Final Clarification Regarding the Dead Sea Sect," *RQ,* V (1964/66):81–87; S. Zeitlin, "History, Historians, and the Dead Sea Scrolls," *JQR,* NS LV (1964/65):97–116; D. Winston, "The Iranian Component in the Bible, Apocrypha, and Qumran: A Review of the Evidence," *History of Religions,* V (1965):183–216; C. Schneider, "Zum Problem des Hellenistischen in den Qumrantexten," *LeipzSymp,* 1963, pp. 299–314; C. Burchard, "Pline et les Esséniens; à propos d'un article récent," *RB,* LXIX (1962):533–97; S. Talmon, "A Further Link between the Judaean Covenanters and the Essenes," *Harvard TR,* LVI (1963):313–19; J. Pryke, "John the Baptist and the Qumran Community," *RQ,* IV (1963/64):483–96; J. Irmscher, "Der Beitrag der neugriechischen Forschung zum Qumranproblem," *LeipzSymp,* 1963, pp. 249–57; S. Segert, "Die Sprachenfrage in der Qumrangemeinschaft," *LeipzSymp,* 1963, pp. 315–39; *idem,* "Sprachliche Bemerkungen zu einigen aramäischen Texten von Qumran," *Archiv Orientálny,* XXXIII (1965):190–206; A. Murtonen, "A Historico-Philological Survey of the Main Dead Sea Scrolls and Related Documents," *Abr-Naharain,* IV (1963/64):56–95.

Calendar: A. Jaubert, "Le calendrier des Jubilés et les jours liturgiques de la semaine," *VT,* VII (1957):33–61; A. Strobel, "Der 22. Tag des XI. Monats im essenischen Jahr," *RQ,* III (1961/62):539–43; S. Zeitlin, "The Judean Calendar during the Second Commonwealth and the Scrolls," *JQR,* NS LVII (1966/67):28–45.

Organization and purpose: W. Tyloch, "Quelques remarques sur le caractère social du mouvement de Qumran," *LeipzSymp,* 1963, pp. 341–51; I. H. Eybers, "Aspekte van die Organisatie en Riten van die Joodse Qumraan-Sekte," dissertation, Pretoria, 1960; W. R. Stegner, "The

JUDAISM OUTSIDE THE HEBREW CANON

Self-Understanding of the Qumran Community Compared with the Self-Understanding of the Early Church," dissertation, Drew, 1960; B. J. Roberts, "Bible Exegesis and Fulfilment in Qumran," *Words and Meanings; Essays Presented to D. Winton Thomas,* 1968, pp. 195–207; P. v. d. Osten-Sacken, "Bemerkungen zur Stellung des Mebaqqer in der Sektenschrift," *ZNW,* LV (1964):18–26; S. T. Kimbrough, Jr., "The Concept of Sabbath at Qumrân," *RQ,* V (1964/66):483–502; M. Delcor, "Repas cultuels esséniens et thérapeutes, Thiases et Haburoth," *RQ,* VI (1967/68):401–25; A. Dupont-Sommer, "Lumières sur l'arrière-plan historique des écrits de Qoumran," *Erets-yisrael,* VIII (1967):25–36; H. Haag, "Das liturgische Leben der Qumrangemeinde," *ArLitg,* X (1967): 78–109; G. Jeremias, *Der Lehrer der Gerechtigkeit,* 1963; K. Schubert, "Der Lehrer der Gerechtigkeit," *WZKM,* LIX/LX (1963/64):137–46; R. A. Rosenberg, "Who is Moreh hasSedeq?" *JAAR,* XXXVI (1968):118–22; R. E. Lilly, *The Idea of Man in Qumran Literature,* 1962; G. W. Buchanan, "The Role of Purity in the Structure of the Essene Sect," *RQ,* IV (1962/63):397–406.

Miscellaneous: J. M. Allegro, *The Dead Sea Scrolls,* 1961; M. Mansoor, *The Dead Sea Scrolls; A College Textbook and a Study Guide,* 1964; H. Haag, *Die Handschriftenfunde in der Wüste Juda,* 1965; R. Meyer, *Das Gebet des Nabonid,* BAL, 107/3, 1962; W. Dommershausen, *Nabonid im Buche Daniel,* 1964; J. Carmignac, "Le recueil de prières liturgiques de la grotte l," *RQ,* IV (1962/63):271–76; J. C. Trever, "Completion of the Publication of Some Fragments from Qumran Cave I," *RQ,* V (1964/66):323–44; J. M. Allegro, *The Treasure of the Copper Scroll,* 1960; R. Meyer, "Die vier Höhlen von Murabba'ât," *ThLZ,* LXXXVIII (1963): 19–28; M. Philonenko, J.-C. Picard, J.-M. Rosenstiehl, F. Schmidt, *Pseudépigraphes de l'Ancien Testament et manuscrits de la Mer Morte,* I, 1967; P. W. Skehan, "The Scrolls and the OT Text," *McCormick Quarterly,* XXI (1967/68):273–83; D. N. Freedman, "The OT at Qumran," *McCormick Quarterly,* XXI (1967/68):299–306.

BHH, III:1537–42 (G. Baumbach); *RGG,* V:740–56 (M. Burrows, R. de Vaux, R. Meyer, K. G. Kuhn, C.-H. Hunzinger); Eissfeldt, pp. 864–74 (English: 637–44); *IDB,* I:790–802 (O. Betz).

In the spring of 1947, two goatherds from the bedouin Ta'amireh tribe, which dwelt in the desert of Judah, discovered Cave 1 at Khirbet Qumran on the west coast of the Dead Sea not far from Ain Feshka. In it were found several manuscript scrolls wrapped in linen and concealed in clay jars. Through an antiquities dealer in Bethlehem, three of them came into the possession of Mar Athanasius Samuel, the metropolitan of the Syrian Orthodox monastery of St. Mark in Jerusalem, while Eleazar Sukenik acquired two others for the Hebrew University. During subsequent years, other caves containing manuscript fragments were discovered near Khirbet Qumran. The ruins were excavated by R. de Vaux, O.P., and further discoveries were made at additional sites: Wadi Murabba'at and Khirbet Mird; and, within Israeli territory, at the Nahal Se'alim (Wadi Sayyal), Nahal Mishmar (Wadi Mahras), and Nahal Hebar (Wadi Habra); and finally at Masada, the Herodian fortress above the west coast of the Dead Sea.

Thanks to the dry climate, the manuscripts suffered very little from moisture and the ravages of rodents and insects during their nineteen hundred years of concealment. An amazing wealth of material came to light, dating (as it turned out) from the second century B.C. to the first half of the first century C.E. Biblical material was also uncovered. A few manuscripts were written on papyrus, but for the most part we are dealing with parchment scrolls, the longest measuring twenty-eight feet.

The manuscripts and fragments contain: (1) texts of all the books in the Hebrew Old Testament Canon (with the exception of the Book of Esther), some in several copies; (2) a series of books belonging to the Greek Canon (the Apocrypha) in their original Hebrew or Aramaic, such as

Sirach and Tobit; (3) a series of pseudepigrapha such as the Book of Jubilees, the Testament of Levi, and the Testament of Naphtali; (4) previously unknown works belonging to none of these categories, ascribed to the Qumran people on the basis of their internal affinities; and (5) business documents, contracts, and letters, primarily from the period of the Jewish revolt (A.D. 67–70) and the Hadrianic revolt (A.D. 132–35 [Wadi Murabba 'at]) down to the Arab period (Khirbet Mird). Here we are concerned only with the manuscripts and fragments belonging to the fourth category, since those in the first category are outside the scope of this book and those of the second and third categories have already been dealt with in the context of the Apocrypha and pseudepigrapha.

The manuscripts that are almost complete, even though damaged, are: (*a*) the Community Rule or Manual of Discipline; (*b*) the Thanksgiving Scroll; (*c*) the Book of the War Between the Sons of Light and the Sons of Darkness (War Scroll); (*d*) the Pesher on Habakkuk; (*e*) the Genesis Apocryphon; and (*f*) the recently discovered Temple Scroll, for which there are only preliminary reports. There are also fragments of the Damascus Document, published by S. Schechter in 1910 on the basis of large fragments found in the genizah of the Ezra Synagogue at Fustat (Old Cairo). In addition, there are fragments, in part unpublished, of many manuscripts exhibiting more or less close affinity with the texts just mentioned. For example, fragments of what may be earlier recensions of the War Scroll and the Community Rule have been discovered. Alongside the Habakkuk Commentary—or, more, accurately, the Habakkuk Pesher—there are remnants of pesharim on Isaiah, Hosea, Micah, Nahum, Zephaniah, and Psalms 37, 57, and 68; it seems probable that these commentaries dealt with individual sections of the prophetical books that could be interpreted with reference to the actual situation of the sect. Above all there are numerous fragments of cultic and liturgical texts that indicate a lively interest in the proper liturgical performance of ceremonial worship. Further study is needed to determine whether these texts represent earlier material adopted by the group or fresh creations and reformulations. It does not appear possible to reduce the various texts and formularies to a single denominator. The only point on which the Qumran discoveries seem to agree is in presupposing the solar calendar of the sect.

The material from Qumran constitutes the bulk of the manuscripts and fragments that have been brought to light since 1947 by bedouin and archeological expeditions in the desert of Judah. In addition, discoveries have been made at Wadi Murabba'at, Khirbet Mird, and Masada. In our discussion of the groups presumably responsible for these literary productions, it is convenient to begin with the minor sites.

Masada was built as a palace fortress by Herod I (37–4 B.C.), and it served as a strong point for the Zealots from A.D. 66 to 73. To the extent that we are concerned with letters and documents, all the finds date from the final years of the struggle against the Romans. The Sirach fragment, however, written in stichs, dates from the first quarter of the first century B.C. (F. M. Cross).

The two caves in Wadi Murabba'at served as strong points during the Bar Kochba revolt. This means that the letters and documents, some of which bear dates, belong to the first third of the second century C.E., while the remaining biblical manuscripts discovered in association with them are earlier.

In the case of Khirbet Mird, we are dealing with the Christian monastery Marda. The discoveries made there include biblical books, as well as Christian texts and documents, in Christian Aramaic, Greek, and Arabic, dating from the fifth to the eighth centuries C.E. Apart from an Aramaic book of Joshua, a Greek fragment of the Wisdom of Solomon deserves special mention. It is clear that at Khirbet Mird the remains of the monastic library and archives have come to light; it is noteworthy that these include a fragment of Euripedes' *Andromache*.

JUDAISM OUTSIDE THE HEBREW CANON

With the exception of the Sirach fragment from Masada and the Greek fragment of the Wisdom of Solomon from Khirbet Mird, none of the Apocrypha or pseudepigrapha have been found at the minor sites in the desert of Judah.

As has been shown above, the situation at Qumran is different. The finds include Hebrew remnants of Enoch, the Testaments of Levi and Naphtali, and Jubilees. Fragments of an Aramaic version of Jubilees have also been found. There are also fragments of several manuscripts of the Damascus Document, discovered in 1896 by S. Schechter in the genizah of the Ezra Synagogue at Fustat (Old Cairo), as well as a wealth of other written materials. Certain problems associated with these will now be discussed before we pass on to some of the major manuscripts.

The manuscripts were found in caves in the first terrace above the surface of the Dead Sea; Khirbet Qumran is also located on this terrace. The excavations of the ruin reveal a complex of buildings with several courtyards and a complicated water supply system including numerous cisterns, usually rectangular, the largest of which was accessible by means of a stairs at one end. The upper story of the main building contained a scriptorium with tables and benches made of clay; many scholars assume that the majority of the manuscripts were written here. A room adjacent to several cisterns, with a small side room for a pantry, served as a refectory and probably as an assembly hall and center for worship, also. The settlement included several workshops. Near it lay a cemetery with some one thousand tombs arranged in rows, none of which contained funerary offerings. The size of the cemetery is out of all proportion with the small building complex.

Apart from a period between about 31 B.C. and A.D. 4, when there was an interruption due to a great earthquake, the site was occupied from shortly before 100 B.C. to A.D. 68. Capture by the Romans put an end to the settlement. A later period of occupation by a Roman outpost is irrelevant in this context.

162

Sixteen caves in the near vicinity concealed the manuscripts or showed traces of occupation. Pottery finds in the building complex and the manuscript caves demonstrate their association. The nonbiblical manuscripts display a uniform, albeit more or less highly differentiated, didactic structure, which can be observed very clearly in, for example, the Manual of Discipline (1QS). Their characteristic divergences from the teachings of the Sadducees and the Pharisees consist of a particularly strict construction of the Law, an extension of priestly regulations governing ritual cleanness and ablutions to the laity under priestly direction, a solar calendar of fifty-two weeks (364 days) instead of a lunar calendar, and a rigorous doctrine of predestination associated with a dualism immediately subordinate to God. These features agree for the most part with the brief statements of Josephus about the Essenes. This would mean that we should see in Qumran a settlement of this sect, known also to Pliny the Elder (*Hist. nat.* v. 15. 73), and assume that when the Romans were on the verge of attacking they collected all their manuscripts throughout the area and hid them in caves near their desert settlement. The hypothesis of a genizah (H. E. del Medico and others) is ruled out (R. de Vaux). K. H. Rengstorf has suggested that the manuscripts represent the temple library concealed for protection; but this hypothesis seems dubious, since the extrabiblical literature, despite all its differences, exhibits the same special teachings, whereas, for instance, there is no trace of mishnaic influence.

Some manuscripts, such as the Pesher on Habakkuk, the Pesher on Psalm 37, and the Damascus Document, make mention of specific events and persons important to the sect. These include the Teacher of Righteousness, the Godless Priest, the Prophet of Lies, and the House of Absalom. Many attempts have been made to identify the particular persons referred to. The "Godless Priest" probably refers to the high priest Jonathan, who held this office from 153 to 143, for the statements indicating he fell into the hands of his enemies and was slain apply to him. The other figures cannot be identified, since, apart from the allusions made to them in the Qumran documents, there are no concrete statements on which to base any hypothesis. G. Jeremias, H. W. Kuhn, and other scholars have suggested that several passages from the Thanksgiving Scroll (1QH ii. 1-9; ii. 31-39; iii. 1-18; iv. 5–v. 4; v. 5-19; v. 20–vii. 5; vii. 6-25; and viii. 4-40) are to be ascribed to the Teacher of Righteousness. This hypothesis gives us an insight into the inward struggles and outward conflicts of the Teacher of Righteousness but does not furnish any concrete data that would make it possible to identify a known historical figure with this founder of the sect who seems to take center stage at Qumran. This approach merely allows us to conclude that the founder exercised his ministry around the middle of the second century B.C. It is reasonable to suppose that we are dealing with a splinter group or successor of the Hasidim movement. The striking breadth of interest exhibited by the Qumran documents suggests that during the roughly two hundred years of the sect's existence, people with a wide variety of views and goals were able to find a home within it so long as they did not call the sect's basic principles into question.

With regret that many texts preserved in too fragmentary condition must be ignored in this introduction, we shall now turn to a more detailed discussion of the major texts.

Community Rule

Text: M. Burrows, with the assistance of J. C. Trever and W. H. Brownlee, *The Dead Sea Scrolls of St. Mark's Monastery, II/2: Plates and Transcription of the Manual of Discipline*, 1951; *DJD*, I:107–30, pl. xxii–xxix.

Translations: Bardtke I, 2nd ed., 1953, pp. 86–110; Bardtke II, 1958, pp. 283–88; M. Burrows, *The Dead Sea Scrolls*, 1956, pp. 371–89; *idem, More Light on the Dead Sea Scrolls*, 1958, pp. 393–98; Maier, I, 1960, pp. 21–45; P.

Wernberg-Møller, *The Manual of Discipline*, 1957; A. Dupont-sommer, pp. 88–127; J. Carmignac, E. Cothenet, and H. Lignée, *Autour de la Bible: Les textes de Qumran, traduits et annotés*, II, 1963:9–64; E. Lohse, *Die Texte aus Qumran, hebräisch und deutsch, mit masoretischer Punktation, Übersetzung, Einführung und Anmerkungen*, 1964; A. R. C. Leaney, *The Rule of Qumran and its Meaning*, New Testament Library, 1966; J. Licht, מגילת הסרכים ממגילות מדבר יהודה, 1965.

Monographs: M. Delcor, "Manual de disciplina (1QS 9,18)," *EncBib*, IV, 1965:1248–50; Y. Baer, "סרך היחד תעידה יהודית ונוצרית לתחילת המאה השניה לספנה," *Tsiyon*, XXIX/1–2 (1964):1–60, i–ii; S. H. Siedl, *Qumran; eine Mönchsgemeinde im Alten Bund; Studie über Serek ha-Yahad*, 1963; C. H. Hunzinger, "Beobachtungen zur Entwicklung der Disziplinarordnung der Gemeinde von Qumran," *LeipzSymp*, 1962, pp. 231–47; M. Weise, *Kultzeiten und kultischer Bundesschluß in der "Ordensregel" vom Toten Meer*, 1961; R. Meyer, "Melchisedek von Jerusalem und Moresedek von Qumran," *SVT*, XV (1966):228–39; B. W. Dombrowski, "יחד in 1QS and *tò koinòn*: An Instance of Early Greek and Jewish Synthesis," *HarvTR*, LIX (1966):294–307.

BHH, III:1760–61 (U. Becker); *RGG*, V:1666–68 (H. Braun); Eissfeldt, pp. 874–80 (English: 645–49).

Text

The Community Rule was discovered in the form of a parchment scroll in Cave 1 at Qumran. The term 1QS is used to denote a single scroll containing eleven columns, the last of which ends in the middle of the page; 1QS[a] designates two columns originally belonging to 1QS, now separate, broken off through wear with some textual loss; and 1QS[b] represents five columns originally appended to 1QS, preserving in damaged fragments the remnants of at least six columns. In addition, Caves 4 and 5 have produced fragments of twelve other manuscripts of the Community Rule, some of which contain interesting variants.

Title

An endpaper fastened to the reverse of column 1 so that it can read without opening the scroll gives the title: [סר]ך היחד ומן, "[Ru]le of the Community; and from . . ."; this title probably includes the appendices 1QSᵃ and 1QSᵇ. The scroll has received a wealth of designations in the secondary literature: Community Rule, Sectarian Scroll, Sectarian Rule, and Manual of Discipline, among others. These terms apply to the first portion, 1QS. The first appendix, 1QSᵃ, is usually called simply "Appendix to the Community Rule"; the second has been called "Prayers, Benedictions." No Hebrew title for either of these appendices has been preserved.

Contents

A brief survey of each scroll fragment by column and line will outline the content of the work as a whole.

1QS

i. 1-15: Superscription and introduction. i. 16–iii. 12: Ritual for the annual renewal of vows and admission of new members. iii. 13–iv. 1: Subdualistic doctrine of the two spirits. iv. 2-8: Acts of the good spirit. iv. 9-14: Acts of the evil spirit. iv. 15-26: Continued existence of the two spirits until the last judgment. v. 1–vi. 23: Basic regulations for the community. vi. 24–viii. 19: Judicial process and punishments for transgressing the regulations. viii. 20–ix. 11: Judicial process in cases of deliberate transgression of the Law of Moses, coupled with assurances that the Law will endure until there appear a prophet and the messiahs Aaron and Israel. ix. 13-21: Directives for the instructor. ix. 21–x. 8: Appropriate observance of seasons, festivals, and the calendar. x. 9–xi. 22: Concluding psalm.

1QSᵃ

i. 1-3: A superscription, including the statement that what is written applies to the whole congregation of Israel until the eschaton. i. 4-5: Assembly to hear the ordinances of the covenant read. i. 6-19: Education of the young; and the age at which members of the congregation are eligible for various offices. i. 19-22: Employment of the feeble-minded. i. 22-25: Levites. i. 25–ii. 11: Admission to the assembly. ii. 11-22: Order of precedence, with the messiah following the priests in the assembly of the congregation and at table.

1QS^b

Of at least six original columns, portions of five have been preserved. They are records of prayers (including benedictions) for the congregation, the high priest, the priests, and the prince of the congregation (נשיא העדה), each with an introductory superscription.

Unity

J. T. Milik points out that two papyrus manuscripts from Cave 4, written in an earlier script dated by F. M. Cross in the beginning of the first century B.C., contain a different and somewhat shorter text of column v. A. R. C. Leaney uses this observation to suggest that the text was made more precise with the passage of time or went through several redactions. In columns vii, viii, and x, 1QS also exhibits traces of editorial revision, such as numerous erasures and corrections; in columns vii and viii, these increase the severity of the stipulated punishments, while in column x they represent textual changes. This probably indicates that in the list of punishments we are dealing with regulations whose laxity appeared questionable to a more rigorous party that arose in the course of time. Thus, they came to be restated.

A more important point is that the passage outlining the hypotheistic dualism of the sect, introduced with the phrase "for the instructor" (evidently the instructor was a respected figure responsible for doctrinal matters), was apparently a finished unit before its incorporation into the

167

Rule. The hymn in columns x and xi probably was originally intended for another purpose.

The first appendix, 1QSᵃ, became necessary when the present situation of the monastic community ceased to be the community's sole interest and its members realized that at the end of days the entire people of Israel, male and female, would join the sect. For the preparatory period leading up to the age of salvation, which the Old Testament said would take place upon this earth, a program of reeducation was considered necessary, beginning with the children. At the same time, an attempt was made to guarantee the prerogatives of the priests over and above the messiah of Israel.

The prayers or benedictions of the second appendix, 1QSᵇ, constitute another independent unit. One view holds that they were used during the lifetime of the sect; another (less likely) view holds that they were meant to apply to the age of salvation.

Place and Date

As the multiplicity of manuscripts suggests, in the Community Rule we have a document of great importance to the Qumran sect; it was intended to define, at least for a certain period, their doctrine and the ordering of the common life lived by this monastic community. It is therefore reasonable to ascribe the Rule to the founder of the community, who is not mentioned in 1QS itself but appears in the Damascus Document as מורה היחד (יורה) (CD B xx. 1, 14). Such an order might have been sketched in outline before the settlement at Qumran was established; but this would have been done with the intention of finding a site and erecting a building where the plans could be realized. Therefore the earliest recension, which appears to be represented in the fragments of the two papyrus manuscripts, can hardly be dated much after the establishment of the settlement at Qumran, even if these manuscripts were not written until around 130 B.C., as the ductus of the script seems to suggest. The settlement, however, was probably founded under Jonathan (160-143 B.C.) or Simon (143-134 B.C.).

It is conceivable, of course, that the "Teacher" of the order did not emerge as the theoretician of the group until after it had been founded under the leadership of someone else, whereupon he gave the stamp of his own personality to the group through his work and, likewise, gave it its name. This hypothesis, however, seems less appropriate than the hypothesis that ascribes the foundation of the settlement to the Teacher; in any case, the settlement presupposes a strong will and considerable resources.

Significance

The Community Rule gives us an insight into the teachings and way of life of a splinter group within late Judaism. It was established by priests probably belonging to the family of the high priest. Through strict observance of the Law, especially the regulations governing ritual purity for the priests, it sought to require the laity who asked to join of their own free will to observe the priestly regulations and, apparently, to accept celibacy or continence within marriage. The purpose of this asceticism was to cause the members of the group to take seriously the imminent expectation of the day of salvation, nourished as it was on contemporary interpretation of the prophetical writings, assuring them that they would thereby reserve a place in the kingdom of light.

Damascus Document

Text: S. Schechter, *Documents of Jewish Sectaries, Vol. I: Fragments of a Zadokite Work*, 1910; L. Rost, *Die Damaskusschrift*, KlT, 167, 1933; S. Zeitlin, *The Zadokite Fragments; Facsimile of the Manuscripts in the Cairo Geniza Collection in the Possession of the University Library, Cambridge, England,* JQR Monograph Series, 1, 1952; C. Rabin, *The Zadokite Document*, 2nd ed., 1958; fragments in *DJD*, III:128–31, 181, pl. xxvi, xxxviii.

Translations: Charles, II:785–834; Riessler, pp. 920–41; Bardtke II, pp. 259–76; Burrows I, pp. 349–64; Dupont-Sommer, pp. 129–56, 163–78; Gaster, pp. 71–94, 108–13; Habermann, pp. 77–88; Maier, I, pp. 46–70; II, pp. 40–62; W. Staerk, *Die jüdische Gemeinde des Neuen Bundes in Damaskus,* BFChrTh, 27/3, 1922; J. Schousboe, *La secte juive de l'alliance nouvelle au pays de Damas et le Christianisme naissant,* 1942.

Monographs: A. Dupont-Sommer, "'Le chef des rois de Jâwân' dans l'Ecrit de Damas," *Sem,* V (1955):41–57; P. A. Quanbeck, "The Use of the OT in the Damascus Document Compared with Normative Judaism and the Synoptic Gospels," dissertation, Princeton Theological Seminary, 1958; R. F. Collins, "The Cairo Damascus Covenant, its Origin and Covenant Notion," dissertation, Louvain, 1962; *idem,* "The Berîth-Notion of the Cairo Damascus Covenant and its Comparison with the NT," *ETL,* XXXIX (1963):555–94; I. Rabinowitz, "The Meaning and Date of 'Damaskus' Document IX. 1," *RQ,* VI (1967/68):433–35.

BHH, I:314–15 (G. Baumbach); *RGG,* II:24–25 (L. Rost); Eissfeldt, pp. 880–84, 1026 (English: 649–52, 777); *IDB,* IV:929–33 (O. Betz).

Text

In 1896, S. Schechter discovered, among the remains of other manuscripts in the genizah of the Ezra Synagogue in Old Cairo, sixteen pages of one manuscript and a single sheet of another. The latter, somewhat larger in format, contained an untitled work in Hebrew previously unknown. Both derived from the ninth or tenth century. Fragments of at least nine manuscripts of the same work have been found in Caves 2, 4, 5, and 6 at Qumran.

Title

In 1910, Schechter published the texts of the untitled work he had discovered, calling them "Fragments of a Zadokite Work," since the work placed special emphasis on the descent of the priests from Zadok. The term "Damascus Document" has also gained currency, since the group addressed is called the "people of the new covenant in the land of Damascus" (viii. 21).

Manuscripts

There are two manuscripts from the Cairo Genizah; the longer is called A, the single leaf, B. Rabin and others have attempted to conflate the two overlapping manuscripts, but such attempts have been unsuccessful; the two manuscripts parallel each other for a while but then diverge. Following a series of scriptural quotations (differing in the two manuscripts), one breaks off, whereas the other suddenly turns into an historical narrative that exhibits close affinities with the Community Rule (1QS). Some of the fragments from the Qumran Caves parallel recension A; others preserve supplementary material not found at Cairo; others must come from an introductory section of text A; still others contain the lost conclusion.

Contents

Text A contains an exhortation introduced by ועתה, (meaning "and now") embellished with historical retrospects and scriptural quotations. It is addressed to a group living in internal exile led by Zadokite priests. It breaks off in mid-sentence (i–viii). Sections ix–xvi, badly worn and only partly legible, contain a kind of mishnah with sabbath regulations, laws governing ritual purity, and directives on the organization of the group in camp and jurisdiction. Leaf B begins with vii. 5 of manuscript A, and then soon passes over to a sketch of the group's history and an eschatological prospect. Of the Qumran fragments, only those from cave 6 have been published; all but one appear to be identical with manuscript A, while the one exception contains a supplement to the mishnah section of manuscript A.

Place and Date

When Schechter published the Cairo texts, estimates of the date of the Damascus Document ranged from the second century B.C. (E. Meyer and others) to the eighth century C.E. (A. Büchler, W. Bousset, and others). The appearance of the fragments at Qumran forces a dating prior to the destruction of this settlement in the Jewish War around A.D. 68. The prototype of A should probably be dated sometime after the middle of the second century B.C., while B probably came into being during the first century B.C. or the early years of the first century C.E. At any event it came into existence before the fortress of the Qumran sect was destroyed, since there is no mention of this catastrophe, which apparently led to the dissolution of the group.

It may be considered certain that the Damascus Document was written in Palestine or its near vicinity. What remains uncertain is whether the repeated mentions of Damascus (vi. 5, 19; vii. 15, 19; viii. 21; xix. 34; and xx. 12) refer to the Nabatean Kingdom or to the environs of Damascus itself—or whether they are merely a fictional representation of an internal emigration.

Author

Schechter and some others thought the author was a Sadducee; E. Meyer, H. Preisker, and others considered him a Pharisee. H. L. Strack thought he could see a Dosithean in the author; G. Margoliouth, a Jewish Christian; and A. Büchler, W. Bousset, and A. Marmorstein, a precursor of the Karaite movement. It is highly likely that there was a late association between this corpus and the Karaites; originally, however, the voice heard was that of one of the Jewish groups that split off under Zadokite leadership, probably in opposition to the gradually stabilized rule of the Maccabees. Possibly this occurred after the office of high priest was transferred to Jonathan, an act some circles considered usurpation. By strict observance of the Law this group hoped to hasten the coming of the messianic age. According to text B, they tried to win over the Qumran group when the latter had become leaderless through the death of the Teacher of the community. This means that the Teacher of Righteousness referred to as the spiritual leader of the Damascus community is later than the teacher of the Community Rule and, therefore, probably belongs to the last third of the first century B.C., if not the beginning of the first century C.E. He may be associated with the resettlement of Qumran after the hiatus of the earthquake.

Significance

The two recensions of the work illustrate the type of post-Maccabean movements within Judaism that paved the way for the Baptist and Jesus—with this important difference—here a group of laymen make themselves subject to the regulations governing the ritual purity of the priests serving in the Temple and practice strict obedience to the Law in order to guarantee that they will live on in the age of salvation, whereas with the preaching of Jesus, a lay movement arises that is independent of priestly requirements.

War Scroll

Text: E. L. Sukenik, *The Dead Sea Scrolls of the Hebrew University*, pls. 16–34; *DJD*, I:135–36, pl. xxxi; Y. Yadin, מגילת מלחמת בני אור בבני חושך, 1957.

Translations: Bardtke II, pp. 215–33; H. A. Brongers, *De Rol van de Strijd*, 1960; Burrows I, pp. 390–99; J. Carmignac, *La Règle de la Guerre des Fils du Lumière contre les Fils de Ténèbres*, 1958; J. Carmignac and P. Guilbert, I:81–125 (J. Carmignac); Dupont-Sommer, pp. 179–211; Gaster, pp. 261–84, 293–98; Habermann, pp. 95–108; Maier, I:123–48, II:111–36; J. van der Ploeg, *Le Rouleau de la Guerre, Traduit et Annoté avec une Introduction*, 1959; Sutcliffe, pp. 204–33; Y. Yadin, *The Scroll of the War of the Sons of Light Against the Sons of Darkness*, 1962; V. M. Vellas, *Ek tōn cheirográphōn tēs Nekrās thalássēs: tò biblíon toū polémou tōn huiōn toū phōtòs katà tōn huiōn toū skótous*, 1965.

JUDAISM OUTSIDE THE HEBREW CANON

Monographs: B. Gärtner, "Bakgrunden till Qum-ranförsamlingens krig," *Religion och Bibel*, XIX (1960):35 ff.; J. Peter Asmussen, "Das iranische Lehnwort *naḫšīr* in der Kriegsrolle von Qumran," *AcOr*, XXVI (1961):3–20; J. M. P. van der Ploeg, "Zur literarischen Komposition der Kriegsrolle," *LeipzSymp* 1963, pp. 293–98; B. Jongeling, *Le Rouleau de la Guerre des mss de Qumran* (StSN, 4), 1964; A. M. Gazov-Ginsberg, "The Structure of the Army of the Sons of Light," *RQ*, V (1965): 163–76; J. Strugnell, "Notes on 1QS 1.17-18; 8.3-4 and 1QM 17.8-9," *CBQ*, XXIX (1967):580–82; P. von der Osten-Sacken u. vom Rhein, *Gott und Belial* (StUNT, 6), 1969.

BHH, III:1539 (G. Baumbach); *RGG,* IV:944–46 (C. H. Hunzinger); Eissfeldt, pp. 885–87 (English: 652–54).

Text

In Qumran Cave 1 a leather scroll was discovered. Some nine and one half feet long, the scroll was made up of five leaves, the first four of which contained eighteen columns; on what is left of the fifth leaf, remnants of a nineteenth column are visible. There is no way to tell whether there were additional columns. The beginning of the scroll is extant, having been protected by sixteen inches of blank leather. Only the lower edge of the scroll exhibits major damage, the loss being two to three lines. Most of the few lacunae can be filled in with little difficulty. Four fragments of four other manuscripts of either this work or an earlier recension have been found in Cave 5.

Title

Unlike the Community Rule, the War Scroll does not contain a colophon, nor does it have an outside label. The first words of the manuscript have been lost, and there are two possible ways of filling the gap to supply the title of the work: וז]ה סדר סרך[המלחמה, "and th[is is the rule for the ordering] of the war"; or וז]ה ספר סרך[המלחמה, "and th[is is the book of the rule] of the war." The title continues: "of the beginning of the fray of the sons of light, to begin with the lot of the sons of darkness." The work used to be cited as DSW; the newer abbreviation is 1QM. The common English title is "War Scroll."

Contents and Structure

The War Scroll comprises a compendium of both military science and the cultic ceremonies to be observed during a war, with special reference to the eschatological battle that will precede the age of salvation. The following sections may be distinguished: i. 1-7—introduction; i. 8-17—the final goal of God's history with his people; ii. 1-14—provisions for worship during the war and organization of the troops, together with a list of foes; ii. 15–iii. 11—directions concerning the use of the priests' trumpets in battle and the inscriptions on them; iii. 12–v. 2—regulations concerning the standards of the community, their structure, their inscriptions, and their length; v. 3–ix. 9—the order of battle, how the different sections are to be armed, and how the priests commit them to battle by means of trumpet signals; ix. 10–18—changes in the order of battle and names of the towers; x. 1–xix. 13—prayers, blessings, and curses to be pronounced by the high priest before, during, and after the battle, with precise instructions for their scheduled use.

The War Scroll describes both the eschatological war that will last forty years and the final defeat of all enemies, especially the final enemy, the Kittim (in fact the inhabitants of Citium on Cyprus, then the Hellenistic empires of the Diadochi, and finally the Romans), then describes the inauguration of God's reign. There is no suggestion of any messianic expectation. The course of battle, with the assistance of the angels (four of whom are mentioned by name—Michael, Gabriel, Sariel, and Raphael), leads finally to total victory after many reverses, provided that the chief priest (high priest) and the other priests carefully carry out their allotted functions, such as sounding the trumpets, praying, and exhorting the people to strengthen their wills. Detailed descriptions are given for the inscriptions and employment of the trumpets and standards, the order of battle, and the arms and duties of the different types of troops. Appropriate note is taken of the regulations contained in the Torah.

Unity

Columns xvff. give the impression of repeating earlier sections. This observation has led Dupont-Sommer and Gaster to treat this second sections (cols. xv–xix) as an appendix to the first section, representing a revision at the hand of a different author. Van der Ploeg, on the other hand, on the basis of clearly demonstrable repetitions and discrepancies (as in the number and names of the priestly trumpets), claims to be able to recognize an earlier recension that was later revised and expanded. He finds the earlier version in the following sections: column i, in whole or at least in part, and columns xv–xix, with the possibility that the prayer of the high priest in x–xii, in whole or in part, followed xv. 5 in the original text. In other words, he considers columns i–xiv a later revision and expansion of the text. Von der Osten-Sacken also thinks in terms of a basic document embellished through expansion, parallel revision, and interpolation.

Date and Place

The date assigned to composition varies according to how the document is interpreted, more precisely according to whether the Kittim are to be understood as the Seleucid Syrians or the Romans. The latter interpretation has been espoused by several scholars, especially Yadin, on the basis of impressive evidence; others have disputed him and supported the contrary opinion, including Van der Ploeg and Von der Osten-Sacken. Yadin assigns to the work a late date—after the appearance of Pompey in Palestine (68 B.C.)—even considering it possible that the work did not come into being until the first half of the first century C.E. Van der Ploeg would prefer to date the earlier version of the War Scroll, columns i and xv–xix, in the early

Maccabean period, while assigning the expanded recension that enlarged the Scroll to its present compass to the second half of the first century B.C. Von der Osten-Sacken even considers it possible to place the initial composition before the appearance of the Maccabees.

The work came into being in Palestine, the expanded recension possibly at Qumran itself. It is nevertheless striking that twice in the Hebrew text we encounter a Persian loanword that had found a place in Aramaic, while even tactical details and technical weapons terminology are expressed in Hebrew.

Author

The author stands clearly at the summit of the military science of his day; not only is he familiar with military theory, as his statements about what horses are most suitable for battle vi. 10-11 show, for example, but he also seems acquainted with actual practice. Since he also has the technical knowledge to discuss the liturgical prayers, he may have been a war priest (הכוהן החרוץ למועד נקם [xv. 6]). He may have been a member of the community whose organization was governed by the Community Rule (1QS, Sᵃ, Sᵇ), or even of the Community of the New Covenant of the Land of Damascus (CD). Neither possibility can be maintained or denied with certainty, since his pregnant language never mentions such important identifying features as the messiahs of Aaron and Israel. What is certain is that neither the style of the Community Rule (1QS) nor that of the Damascus Document is identical with the style of the author of the War Scroll, although Von der Osten-Sacken has demonstrated the influence of both, as well as affinities with I Maccabees.

Significance

The War Scroll is a hybrid combining a sober military handbook with an apocalypse, the latter looking forward to an eschaton inaugurated by a war lasting forty years, albeit without any messiah or speculative cosmology, together with the preparations for this war, conceived as a systematically organized campaign within the biblical Near East and the Mediterranean world. It stands apart from the milieu of the Community Rule and the Damascus Document (characterized by extreme observance of the Law) especially in its regulations governing ritual purity, and also from the fantastic speculations of the actual apocalypses. Within the corpus of post-Maccabean literature it is a unique representative of an interesting genre.

Pesher on Habakkuk

Text: M. Burrows (with the assistance of J. C. Trever and W. H. Brownlee), *The Dead Sea Scrolls of St. Mark's Monastery; I: The Isaiah Manuscript and the Habakkuk Commentary,* 1950, pp. xix–xxi, pls. lv–lxi; F. A. W. van't Land and A. S. van der Woude, *De Habakukrol van 'Ain Fasha; Tekst en Vertaling,* 1954.

Translations: Bardtke I, pp. 125–31; Burrows, 1956, pp. 365–70; 1957, pp. 303–308; J. Cantera Ortiz de Urbina, *El Comentario de Habacuc de Qumran,* 1960; Dupont-Sommer, pp. 270–80; Gaster, pp. 235–41, 249–53; Habermann, pp. 37–49; Maier, I:149–56, II:137–51; B. M. Vellas, *Tò hypómnēma eis tò biblíon toū Abbakouk,* 1958; E. Lohse, *Die Texte aus Qumran, hebräisch und deutsch,* 1964.

Monographs: K. Elliger, *Studien zum Habakkuk-Kommentar vom Toten Meer,* 1953; K. M. T. Atkinson, "The Historical Setting of the Habakuk Commentary," *JSSt,* IV (1959):238–63; F. F. Bruce, "The Dead Sea Habakkuk Scroll," *AnLeedsUOS,* I (1959):5–24; J. Carmignac, "Notes sur les Peshârim," *RQ,* III (1961/62):505–38; P. Wallendorff, *Rättfärdighetens Lärare,* 1964.

BHH, III:1538–42 (G. Baumbach); *RGG,* III:4–6 (K. Elliger); Eissfeldt, pp. 891–96, 1026–27 (English: 657–61; 777–78).

Text

The Pesher on Habakkuk was discovered in Cave 1. It is a leather scroll 4.7 feet long, written in thirteen columns of varying width. The final column contains only four lines, representing the end of the scroll. The bottom edge has been badly damaged, so that the bottom lines have been lost. The beginning of the scroll is also mutilated, so that the first column is preserved only in fragments.

Title

The original title of the scroll has not been preserved. On the basis of its content, it has been called the Habakkuk Commentary (by Millar Burrows, who first published it) or, more accurately, the Pesher on Habakkuk. It was formerly cited as DSH; its current abbreviation is 1QpH. Elliger suggested the name "Habakkuk Scroll" (HR), but this term has not gained acceptance.

Contents

The scroll contains an interpretation of the first two chapters of the prophet Habakkuk. The text, which diverges only at a few points from the Masoretic text, is divided into paragraphs, each supplied with an interpretation applying it to the history of the Qumran sect. What we are dealing with is therefore more like a contemporary application of the traditional words of the prophet than an interpretation. The term "pesher" (פשר) used by the scroll takes this fact into account.

Biblical Text and Unity

The text departs from the Masoretic at only a few points; the Masoretic is almost always better. The text represented by the Pesher is therefore one of the pre-Masoretic vulgar texts. It may be based on oral tradition or quoted from memory. This could explain the numerous instances of plene orthography, which would be difficult to account for if a manuscript were being carefully copied. One special feature is the use of the archaic Hebrew script for writing the tetragrammaton.

The restriction of the Pesher to the first two chapters of Habakkuk raises a literary question. Was the author of the Pesher familiar with only these chapters, or did he forgo interpreting the third chapter because it was not sufficiently in line with his purposes or because he did not want to apply it to the history of his group?

Date and Place

The author of the commentary was undoubtedly a member of the Qumran sect, who probably belonged to the monastic community. Since he alludes to events that have just taken place, one could follow A. Murtonen in thinking of a date around the end of the second century B.C. That would be the earliest date possible; the beginning of the first century B.C. is also a possibility.

Significance

The scroll gives us an insight into how the group interpreted the writings of the Old Testament prophets and the Psalms, delegating the work to appropriate members. By representing the fates of individual members of the sect and of the sect as a whole as having been predicted by the prophets, this interpretation reveals the necessity of these afflictions, foreseen in God's plan, and makes it possible to overcome them through submission to the will of God and to understand them as transitory stages on the way to the dawn of the age of salvation. The popularity of this type of interpretation is shown by fragments of other pesharim from Qumran interpreting Isaiah, Hosea, Micah, Nahum, Zephaniah, and Psalms 37, 57, and 68. The scanty fragments give insufficient basis for determining whether only isolated passages or major portions of the text were dealt with.

Genesis Apocryphon

Text: N. Avigad and Y. Yadin, *A Genesis Apocryphon from the Wilderness of Judaea*, 1956; *DJD*, I:86–87, pl. xvii.

Translations: Burrows I, pp. 387–93; Dupont-Sommer, pp. 297–306; Gaster, pp. 330–43; Maier, I:157–65, II:152–53.

Monographs: E. Y. Kutsher, "The Language of the 'Genesis-Apocryphon': A Preliminary Study," *Studia Hierosolymitana*, IV (1958):1–35; R. Meyer, "URUK.KI und 'EREK.Mat (Genesis Midrasch II,23)," *RQ*, III (1961/62):553–58; H. H. Rowley, "Notes on the Aramaic of the Genesis Apocryphon," *Festschrift G. R. Driver*, 1963, pp. 116–29; J. A. Fitzmyer, *The Genesis Apocryphon of Qumran Cave I; A Commentary*, 1966; G. J. Kuiper, "A Study of the Relationship between a Genesis Apocryphon and the Pentateuchal Targumim in Gen 14:1-12," *In Memoriam Paul Kahle*, ed. M. Black and G. Fohrer, BZAW, 103, 1968, pp. 149–61.

BHH, III:1538–42 (G. Baumbach); *RGG*, V:744–45 (R. Meyer); Eissfeldt, pp. 900–902 (English: 664–67).

Text

One of the scrolls discovered in Cave 1, acquired by the Syrian Orthodox patriarch and later sold to Israel, turned out when opened to be an Aramaic retelling of Genesis with both the beginning and end missing. Besides fragments that probably represent the initial columns, twenty-two badly damaged columns have been preserved. They are only partially legible, having suffered badly from decay of the leather, chemical reaction of the ink, and other causes. Since column xxii was rolled up at the center and breaks off in mid-sentence, nothing can be said about the original length of the scroll or the compass of the narrative.

Title

Since a separated fragment contained the name Lamech, J. C. Trever assumed that the work was the Book of

Lamech, mentioned in a Greek list of apocryphal writings. When J. Biberkraut opened the scroll, it turned out that only a few words of the first column were legible, not enough to classify it. The second column began with Lamech's alarm at the birth of Noah; the twenty-second concluded with a paraphrase of Genesis 15:14. When Y. Yadin and N. Avigad published it, they therefore called it a Genesis Apocryphon (1QGenApoc).

Contents

The second column, which is legible, begins with Lamech's suspicion that the newborn Noah might have been the product of the activity of the guardian angels or nephilim. He betakes himself to his wife Bitenosh and adjures her by God to tell him the truth. She swears that he is the father of the child. Lamech nevertheless hastens to his father Methuselah, asking him to make inquiry of Enoch. Columns iii and iv are illegible.

In column v, Enoch declares that Lamech, not one of the sons of heaven, is the father of the child, whereupon Methuselah passes on the information to Lamech, who takes cognizance of it. Column vi is badly damaged but clearly contains words spoken by Noah. In column vii (and quite possibly in the totally illegible columns viii and ix) Noah probably tells about the Deluge, since column x speaks of the landing of the ark on Mount Ararat.

All that can be made out in column xi is the statement that the partaking of blood is forbidden. Column xii contains the beginning of the story of Noah the wine-grower, while columns xiii and xiv are indecipherable. In columns xvi and xvii, fragments of the table of nations can be made out, while nothing legible is preserved of column xviii. Column xix tells of the altar at Bethel (?) and the journey to Egypt. Abram tells of a dream he had the night before he entered Egypt, in which he saw a cedar and a date palm. People tried to fell the cedar but left off when the date palm called out a curse on those who would fell the cedar. Terrified, Abram awakes and tells his dream to

Sarah, asking her to pretend that he is not her husband but her brother.

After five years in Egypt, Abram is visited by three dignitaries from Zoan; he welcomes them and reads to them from the Book of the Words of Enoch. In column xx, the visitors extol the beauty of Sarah to Pharaoh in a kind of poetic description (*wasf*) that does not begin to approach the realism and wealth of imagery displayed by corresponding poems in the Song of Songs. Sarah is lodged in the harem of Pharaoh and saves her husband from death by pretending that he is her brother. Abram prays to God and weeps. Gods sends forth an afflicting spirit whose power cannot be broken by physicians. Then Hyrkanos comes to Abram to cause him to intercede for Pharaoh. He is told by Lot about the situation and asked to bring about the return of Sarah. This takes place. Abram prays and lays his hands upon the head of Pharaoh, who is healed. Abram is richly rewarded and sent from Egypt with Sarah and all her possessions.

In column xxi Abram returns to Bethel, offers sacrifice, and gives thanks to God. Then Lot leaves Abram and goes to Sodom. Abram goes to Ramath-Hazor, where he receives the promise of the land. He continues his journeys as far as the Euphrates and finally settles northeast of Hebron. The rest of columns xxi and xxii repeat the content of Genesis 14 with significant variations, followed by the beginning of Genesis 15. The end of the column is reached in the midst of Genesis 15:4; nothing more is preserved.

Genre

The Genesis Apocryphon is a type of narrative literature similar to the Book of Jubilees—which treats the same material—and the Book of Noah in Ethiopic Enoch. Judith and Tobit provide extracanonical parallels; Ruth and Esther provide parallels from the canonical literature. But the Genesis Apocryphon differs from all of these in being composed in the first person. In part the narrative resembles a midrash, in part a kind of targum. The lack of an absolute chronology distinguishes the Apocryphon from Jubilees. Furthermore, the narrative is somewhat flat even in tense situations and never reaches a climax. There is no trace of special emphasis on legal concerns, as there is, for example in Jubilees. The Apocryphon must therefore be classified as an example of popular edifying literature having no recognizable bias.

Date and Place

The year A.D. 68 is the *terminus ante quem*. The work itself suggests the end of the first century B.C. or the first third of the first century C.E. The Aramaic, too, according to E. Y. Kutscher and J. A. Fitzmyer, belongs to this period; thus we may be dealing with the original manuscript.

Author

The somewhat colorless work composed by the author offers no clues as to what group he belonged to within the historical situation. If he wrote, as seems likely, for the edification of extended circles of interested laymen, it is reasonable to suppose that he suppressed the special teachings of his own group. But the conclusion is equally justified that he was unfamiliar with them and therefore did not belong to the inner circle of the Qumran group or groups. The very fact that he made use of Aramaic shows that he sought his audience among the *'am hā'āreṣ*. He can be termed a lay pastor.

Significance

The hypotheses just presented make the retelling of Genesis a work of entertaining edification for the Aramaic-speaking stratum of the uneducated. A striking feature is the marked interest in the problem of what influence can be ascribed to the intervention of the sons of God (Gen. 6:1 ff.) in the affairs of men; it is justifiable to ask whether there are not hints of subtle polemic against mixed marriage. The extensive treatment of the figure of Bitenosh and again of Sarah in Egypt raises the possibility that marriage problems may have occasioned the composition of the work.

Thanksgiving Scroll (Hodayoth)

Text: E. L. Sukenik, *The Dead Sea Scrolls of the Hebrew University*, 1955, pp. 37–39, pl. 35–58; *DJD*, Vol. I, pp. 136–38, pl. xxxi; J. Licht, *The Thanksgiving Scroll; Text, Introduction, Commentary and Glossary*, 1957; M. Delcor, *Les Hymnes de Qumran (Hodayot); Texte Hébreu, Introduction, Traduction, Commentaire*, 1962.

Translations: Bardtke II, pp. 233–58; Burrows I, pp. 400–15; Dupont-Sommer, pp. 213–66; J. Carmignac and P. Guilbert, I:127–280 (J. Carmignac); Gaster, pp. 131–97, 201–17; Habermann, pp. 115–44; M. Mansoor, *The Thanksgiving Hymns; Translated and Annotated with an Introduction*, 1961; A. van Selms, *De Rol der Lofprijzingen vertaald en toegelicht*, 1957; E. F. Sutcliffe, pp. 184–203; S. van der Woude, *De Dankpsalmen*, 1957; P. Rossano, "Hymni ad Mare Mortuum reperti latine redditi," *VD*, XLII (1964):285–99; P. W. Rotenberry, "A Translation and Study of the Qumran Hodayot," dissertation, Vanderbilt, 1968 (*DA*, XXIX [1968/69]:955–56).

Monographs: S. Holm-Nielsen, *Hodayot; Psalms from Qumran*, Acta theologica danica, 2, 1960; G. Morawe, *Aufbau und Abgrenzung der Loblieder von Qumrân*, 1961; *idem*, "Vergleich des Aufbaus der Danklieder und hymnischen Bekenntnislieder (1QH) von Qumran mit dem Aufbau der Psalmen im AT und im Spätjudentum," *RQ*, IV (1962/63):323–54; B. Thiering, "The Poetic Forms of the Hodayoth," *JSSt*, VIII (1963):189–209; J. A. Balbontín, "Los himnos del Maestro de Perfección de Qunran," *Atlántida*, II/11 (1964):538–45; S. J. de Vries, "The Syntax of Tenses and Interpolation in the Hodayoth," *RQ*, V (1964/66):375–414; F. Michelini Tocci, "Qumranica," *Festschrift P. G. Rinaldi*, 1967, pp. 227–38; S. B. Hoenig,

"Readings and Meanings in Hodayot (1QH)," *JQR*, LVIII (1967/68):309–16.

BHH, II:731–32 (A. W. van der Woude); *RGG*, III:387–89 (H. Bardtke); Eissfeldt, pp. 887–91, 1026 (English: 654–57, 777).

Text

Toward the end of 1947, E. L. Sukenik acquired some of the material discovered in Cave 1 at Qumran from a dealer in antiquities, including four leaves and sixty-six fragments of a psalm scroll. The leaves had been folded subsequent to their discovery, either by the Ta'amireh bedouin who discovered them or by the dealer; the fragments had been bundled up. The four badly damaged leaves contained eighteen columns with about thirty-four (according to Dupont-Sommer, Licht, and Mansoor, thirty-two) fragmentary hymns written in the first person (G. Morawe). The fragments probably represent additional columns; fragment 10 is unique in being composed in the first person plural. It is impossible to say anything about the original compass of the scroll. Two hands can be distinguished: one represented by columns i–x and several fragments, the other by columns xiff. and the rest of the fragments. There are also remnants of five leather manuscripts and one papyrus from Cave 4, in which the sequence of hymns sometimes differs. Fragments of five other manuscripts from Cave 4 exhibit a similar style, but their connection with the Thanksgiving Scroll is debatable because there are no identical passages.

Title

No original title or colophon has survived. Since the majority of the hymns begin with the phrase אודכה אדוני (only a few with ברוך אתה אדוני), the title "Hodayot" (הודיות) has gained currency. The usual English designation is "Thanksgiving Scroll" or "Thanksgiving Hymns."

Contents and Genre

The scroll contains hymns composed in a loose *parallelismus membrorum;* the deterioration of the leather often makes it difficult to do more than guess at the physical outlines of individual hymns. Mansoor has identified thirty-two; others have identified up to twice that number. The beginning of each hymn is usually indented, but not always. Sometimes a blank line can be made out between two hymns; sometimes the final line is only a half line. In at least one instance (xi. 32), the phrase ברוך אתה does not introduce a new hymn, but only a new stanza (possibly also xi. 29).

With respect to genre, we are dealing with thanksgiving hymns and hymnic confessions; in comparison to the Psalms they exhibit a plethora of meditative interpolations and reflective passages.

Unity

G. Jeremias has isolated a group of hymns distinguished from the rest by their diction, profundity, and deeply personal tone; he defines this group as: ii. 1-19; ii. 31-39; iii. 1-18; iv. 5–v. 4; v. 5-19; v. 20–vii. 5; vii. 6-25; and viii. 4-40. He thinks they should be ascribed to the towering personality of the Teacher of Righteousness, while considering the others compositions of his followers. This is possible. It is also conceivable that the Teacher of the Community, who may be distinct from the Teacher of Righteousness (CD xx. 1, 14), has here recorded his personal experiences with God in the form of first person psalms.

Author and Date

If the discussion in the preceding paragraph is accurate, the hymns were composed by several authors—the master, whether the Teacher of the Community or the Teacher of Righteousness, and the disciples who followed him and strove to imitate both his spiritual experiences and his way of putting them into words. The master must be dated at the beginning of the movement, probably around the middle of the second century B.C.; his disciples can be dated later. But if the *sēfer hāhāgû* (CD x. 6; xv. 2) or the *sēfer hāhāgî* (1QS^a i. 7) is identical with the hymn scroll, the disciples' work cannot be dated too much later than their master's.

Significance

Within the corpus of the Qumran documents, the Thanksgiving Scroll, despite its borrowing of motifs and images from the canonical Psalter, is the most personal work. It bears witness to the introversion of its author through its restriction of experience to a single person—specifically, that person's coming into being as God's creation, his persecution at the hands of other men, and his trust in God's help until he is received into the circle of the spirits. Outside the context of his people and their history—only alluded to once (in the statement that God spoke through Moses)—the poet praises God and meditates upon God's miraculous governance of his life, despite his creatureliness and his sin.

Temple Scroll

Monographs: Y. Yadin, "The Temple Scroll," *BA*, XXX (1967):135–39; A. Andreassen, "Tempel-Rullen," *Kirke og kultur*, LXXIII (1968):262–67; Shraga Har-Gil, "Das Geheimnis der letzten Rolle; Archäologen entziffern 2000 Jahre alte, immer noch moderne Mobilmachungspläne," *Christ und Welt*, XXI/6 (Feb. 9, 1968), p. 17; J. Jeremias, "Die Tempelrolle," *FAZ*, Feb. 19, 1968 (no. 42), p. 20; Y. Yadin, "Die Tempelrolle; Bericht über die 1967 entdeckte Schriftrolle vom Toten Meer," *FAZ*, Aug. 31, 1968 (no. 202), "Bilder und Zeiten," p. 4.

Text

When the Israelis occupied the city of Bethlehem on June 7, 1967, a scroll some twenty-seven feet long, consisting of sixty-six leaves, came to light; it had been in the possession of Kando, a dealer in antiquities. The beginning is not preserved. It was found in an unidentified cave near the Dead Sea. Paleographical evidence suggests a dating in the first third of the first century C.E.

Title

Yadin called it the Temple Scroll, since thirty of its sixty-eight columns deal with the Temple.

Contents

There are four primary types of material: (1) religious legislation, especially about what is clean and unclean; (2) a list of the offerings and sacrifices for festivals; (3) instructions for the construction of the Temple; (4) regulations for the royal bodyguard and mobilization in the face of a threat from without.

Some of the religious legislation stands in contradiction to the Mishnah, always representing a more rigorous position. The Festival Torah adds to the festivals listed in sections 28 and 29 a festival of new wine and a festival of new oil, the former taking place fifty days after the Feast of Weeks and the latter, fifty days after the former. Since the festival of new oil is to be observed on the twenty-second day of the sixth month, we must be dealing with the solar calendar attested in the other Qumran documents (52 weeks = 364 days + 1 day). The regulations governing construction of the Temple also differ from all known descriptions: the Temple is surrounded by three square concentric courts, each of which is to have twelve gates. The ordinances concerning the king follow Deuteronomy 17:14ff. and refer primarily to the strength of the royal bodyguard and the manner in which they are to venture into battle when danger threatens and there is a direct attack on the land.

Genre

The author's purpose is to compose a discourse as if from the mouth of Yahweh in the style of Deuteronomy. We shall have to await publication of the scroll to understand clearly the relationship of the Temple Scroll to the major Qumran manuscripts.

IV. SUPPLEMENT

AHIKAR

Text: Aramaic—E. Sachau, *Aramäische Papyrus und Ostraka aus einer jüdischen Militärkolonie zu Elephantine*, 1911, T. 40–50; A. Ungnad, *Aramäische Papyrus aus Elephantine*, 1911, pp. 50–63; A. E. Cowley, *Aramaic Papyri of the Fifth Century* B.C., 1923, pp. 204–48. Armenian, Syriac, and Arabic—F. C. Conybeare, J. R. Harris, and A. S. Lewis, *The Story of Ahikar*, 1898.

Translations: Charles, II:715–84; H. Gressmann, *Altorientalische Texte zum AT*, 1926, pp. 454–62; J. B. Pritchard, *Ancient Near Eastern Texts Relating to the OT*, 1950, pp. 427–30 (H. L. Ginsberg).

Monographs: F. Vattioni, "Ancora il vento del nord di Prov 25, 23 [e Aḥiqar syr.]," *Bib*, XLVI (1965):213–16; L. Rost, "Bemerkungen zu Ahiqar," *MIOF*, XV (1969):308–11.

Text

The earliest extant witness to the text is a papyrus fragment from Elephantine, now in Berlin, dating from the end of the fifth century B.C. It was discovered by Dr. Rubensohn during the excavations in 1906–1908 and published by E. Sachau in 1911. A complete text is found in the Syriac version, attested by manuscripts (some of them fragmentary) in Berlin, Cambridge, London, Urmia, and a monastery near Mosul. There is also an Arabic version attested by manuscripts in Berlin, Cambridge, Gotha, Copenhagen, Paris, London, and Rome. Fifteen wisdom proverbs, translated from the Arabic into Ethiopic, have

191

been incorporated into the Book of the Wise Philosopher. An Armenian version dating from around A.D. 450 is found in numerous manuscripts in Edshmiatsin, Oxford, Paris, and Venice, while a portion of the Ahikar narrative, the journey to Egypt, has found its way into the Greek *Life of Aesop*.

Syriac Title

The narrative is entitled "History of Ahikar the Wise."

Contents (Syriac Version)

Ahikar is the wise vizier of Sennacherib. As had been predicted when he was still a child, he remained childless despite the sixty wives he married. He prays for guidance and is instructed to adopt Nadan, the son of his sister. He raises Nadan to succeed him and recommends him to the king, who places him in Ahikar's office. Ahikar instructs Nadan in wisdom to aid in the performance of his office. Nadan, however, takes part in intrigues and, with the aid of forged letters, succeeds in having Ahikar fall from favor and condemned to death by the enraged king. But the official charged with carrying out the sentence owes his life to the sage advice of Ahikar, who had once saved him from the rage of the king's father. Recalling this incident, he takes pity on Ahikar, slays a slave instead, and conceals the out-of-favor Ahikar. The news of Ahikar's death reaches Egypt. Pharaoh thereupon writes to Sennacherib, requesting a master builder who could build him a castle between heaven and earth and answer any question put to him. No one is capable of doing so. Now Sennacherib realizes what an incomparable adviser he had in Ahikar and laments his death, whereupon the intended executioner confesses that he did not carry out his orders and that Ahikar is still alive. Brought before the king, Ahikar declares himself prepared to go to Egypt, where his wise measures and answers win Pharaoh's admiration. Upon his return, he imprisons Nadan in a chamber beneath the door to his house, distracts him with parables, and lets him perish.

192

Variants

Only the most important variants will be mentioned. Of the earliest recension, the version found at Elephantine, only the badly damaged beginning is extant. Ahikar adopts Nadan as his son, whom he presents before Esarhaddon, king of Assyria, as his successor. Nadan traduces his father. The king orders that Ahikar be executed, but Ahikar pleads for his life and the intended executioner instead executes a eunuch, reporting to the king that he has carried out his orders. The proverbial wisdom never exhibits the lapidary *mashal* style of the book of Proverbs and seems not to have made a sharp distinction between parables and proverbs. None of the extant proverbs appear in the other variants of the Ahikar tradition.

All the later variants, whether Syriac, Arabic, or Armenian, agree in making Nadan the son of the sister of Ahikar, who is childless. Ahikar brings up his adopted nephew to succeed him. These texts also agree for the most part in the proverbial material they incorporate, although it is much abbreviated in the Armenian version, and the sequence differs in the Syriac and Arabic. In the Syriac version, the instruction given Nadan before he takes office is in the *mashal* style, mostly one-line aphorisms with a few two-liners. The Arabic and Armenian versions prefer freer forms.

The Arabic and Armenian share an interesting feature: the childless Ahikar first addresses the gods, called in the Armenian Belsim (Baalshem), Simil (Shemesh), and Shamin (Shamen), before calling upon the Most High God.

It cannot be determined with certainty whether the journey to Egypt was part of the original story. This section of the tradition alone is associated with the figure of Aesop and recorded in a Greek *Life of Aesop*.

Date

The material preserved in the Aramaic fragments was probably extant in Akkadian during the Assyrian period, since it mentions Sennacherib and Esarhaddon, and does

193

not contain anything that would contradict this dating. The proverbs, too, are appropriate to the requirements of the fable; with their frequent mention of Shamash or the gods, they too bear the mark of the pre-Persian period. A. E. Cowley and others are probably correct in assigning the translation into Aramaic (accomplished by someone who was not a Jew) to the Persian period, somewhere around the middle of the fifth century.

A Jewish recension can be discerned in Tobit 1:21-23 and 14:10, but it is no longer extant. It made Ahikar the nephew of the elder Tobit and presented the story in such a way that Nadan (in Tobit, Adam) led the man who brought him up out of light into darkness, but God delivered Ahikar and in revenge consigned Nadan to darkness. No trace of this judaized version of the old narrative appears in the later Syriac, Arabic, or Armenian recensions, with their exaggerated embellishment of the material; this means that the judaized version remained a side development, while the extant recensions emphasize the basically non-Jewish nature of the story by speaking of Aramaic and Phoenician gods and ceremonies. The Christian features that appear in the proverbial material at the end of the Syriac recension probably represent the final stage of development; thus the Syriac recension must be dated in the Christian Era, possibly in the second century.

Genre

The story of Ahikar is an example of secular wisdom literature, especially in its earlier Elephantine recension. In the later versions the childless Ahikar prays to God (Syriac), or first the gods, and finally the "Most High God" (Arabic and Armenian). There is no mention of any god in the proverbial wisdom, which is comparable to Egyptian proverb collections in which, as here, a vizier imparts wisdom instruction to his son, who is to be his successor. The unique feature of the Ahikar narrative is its novelistic form. It is a significant example of Semitic secular

194

literature. That it was known in the Aramaic-speaking Jewish colony at Elephantine and gave rise to several later recensions testifies to the popularity of its subject matter.

Pseudo-Philo

Text: G. Kisch, *Pseudo-Philo's Liber antiquitatum biblicarum,* 1949.
Translation: Riessler, pp. 735–861.
Monographs: M. Philonenko, "Remarques sur un hymne essénien de charactère gnostique," *Sem,* XI (1961):43–54.
BHH, III:1460 (B. Reicke); *IDB,* III:795–96 (P. Winter).

Text

Pseudo-Philo has been preserved in Latin translation. G. Kisch lists twenty medieval manuscripts dating from the eleventh to the fifteenth century, all from Germany or Austria. Since all the manuscripts, besides minor variants, exhibit a major lacuna of the approximate compass of a single leaf between chapters 37 and 38, they must (if this mutilation had not already taken place in the Greek text from which the Latin was translated) derive from a lost original. But not even the lost Greek text represents the original version. Diction, imagery, and syntax point to a Hebrew original, which might be reconstructed by retroversion.

Title

The work was first published by Johannes Sichardus (1499–1552), who gave it the title *Philonis Judaei Antiquitatum biblicarum liber.* The Fulda manuscript bears the title *Liber Philonis antiquitatum,* added in the fourteenth century; this title, with minor changes, reappears on other manuscripts. Several eleventh-century manuscripts bear no title; in them the text begins: "*Incipit Genesis. Initium mundi.*" Riessler gives his translation the title "Philo: Das Buch der biblischen Altertümer."

Contents

The work is a retelling of history from Genesis 5 to I Samuel 31:4, with many omissions and novelistic embellishments. It breaks off in the middle of the account of Saul's death. The hypothetical original discussed above, with the large lacuna between chapters 37 and 38, must have ended at this point, either because the rest of the narrative was lost or because the author was prevented from finishing his work.

The contents in outline are: i–vii—the primal history from Genesis 5 to 11, including an extended account of Abraham's deliverance from the fiery furnace, associated with the tower of Babel; viii—Jacob's descendants; ix—the sojourn in Egypt and birth of Moses; x–xix—the Exodus, journey through the desert, revelation at Sinai, the golden calf, and the death of Moses; xx–xxiv—the deeds of Joshua and his farewell discourse; xxv–xxviii—the judge Kenez; xxix–xlviii—the other judges; xlix—Elkanah's refusal of the kingship; l–liii—Samuel's youth (I Sam. 1–3); liv–lv—the story of the ark (I Sam. 4–6); lvi–lvii—Saul's appointment as king (I Sam. 9:1-10); lviii—victory over the Amalekites and Agag (I Sam. 15); lix–lx—the anointing of David and the evil spirit of Saul; lxi—Goliath; lxii—Jonathan's friendship with David; lxiii—the priests of Nob; and lxiv–lxv—the witch of Endor and the battle with the Philistines. With Saul's dying order to the Amalekites to say to David, "Thus says Saul, Do not remember my hatred and my injustice," the narrative breaks off, twice referring the reader to the book of Judges and once to I Samuel for additional information.

Author and Date

The author lived in Palestine, possibly in Jerusalem. He was a Jew. There are no Christian allusions. His discussion of sacrifice is from the perspective of a layman. He had no affinities with Qumran; his position is closer to that of the Pharisees, since he attaches great importance to observance of the Law, though not exhibiting much interest in casuistry. He probably wrote the work shortly after A.D. 70, since in xix. 7 he alludes briefly to the destruction of the Temple after 740 years.

Genre

The work is an example of midrashic retelling of sacred history similar to the Genesis Apocryphon and Jubilees. Within the canonical corpus, it is comparable to P and, above all, Chronicles. As in the latter, great importance is attached to genealogical relationships, listing of names not recorded in sacred tradition, insertion of prayers and hymns, and embellishment of narratives through the addition of unrecorded circumstances and episodes—often with novelistic overtones and complications. It is characteristic of the author to write discourses bringing to light unrecorded facts and stories and to interpret them as examples.

Significance

The work provides interesting insights into how biblical texts were embellished for edification during the first century C.E. At the same time, it illustrates how many acute problems were dealt with by placing the solution in the mouth of a biblical character. The death of Deborah, for example, is used to answer the question of whether one could give a dying man requests for intercession, since he is entering heaven; the power of the heathen gods is illustrated by the temptation of Midian.

The work is skillfully written and obliges pious curiosity without falling into tastelessness. It was taken up by early Christianity and achieved popularity under the pseudonym of Philo in part of the Latin church during the Middle Ages.

Chronological Table

	323 B.C. Death of Alexander the Great at Babylon; his empire disintegrates.
	320–283 B.C. Ptolemy I Soter, ruler of Egypt, gains hegemony over Palestine.
300 B.C.	

Esther
    Judith
    Isaiah 24–27
	283–246 B.C. Ptolemy II Philadelphus; Pentateuch translated into Greek in Alexandria.

200 B.C. Ecclesiastes Baruch (earliest part)	200 B.C. Defeat of the Egyptians at Panium brings Palestine under the hegemony of the Seleucid Antiochus III the Great (222–187).

ca. 190 B.C. Sirach (Hebrew)
    Book of Noah (Eth. Enoch)
    Eth. Enoch 12–16	

	175–164 B.C. Antiochus IV Epiphanes

170 B.C. Apocalypse of Weeks (Eth. Enoch)
    Journey sections of Ethiopic Enoch
    Daniel
    War Scroll (earliest part)
	167–166 B.C. Mattathias, priest at Modein

	166–160 B.C. Judas Maccabeus
	152 B.C. Jonathan (who is not a Zadokite) becomes high priest.

199

Sibyllines (Book 3)
Prayer of the Three
	Young Men
Thanksgiving Scroll
Community Rule
Martyrdom of Isaiah
Zechariah 9–14
Damascus Docu-
	ment A
Bel at Babylon
Testament of Levi
Testament of Naph-
	tali

142 B.C. Simon gains exemption from taxes for
the Jews, thus re-
moving them from
the sovereignty of
the Seleucids and
giving them inde-
pendence.

132 B.C. Sirach (Greek)

ca. 130 B.C. Letter of Aristeas
III Maccabees
Astronomical section
	of Ethiopic Enoch

ca. 130 B.C. First settlement at
Qumran
Animal apocalypse
	section of Ethiopic
	Enoch

ca. 109–
105 B.C. Jubilees
100 B.C. II Maccabees
Pesher on Habakkuk
Additions to Esther
Genesis Apocryphon
Similitudes of Enoch
Wisdom of Solomon
I Maccabees

104 B.C. The high priest Aristobulus assumes the
title "king."

63 B.C. Pompey enters the
holy of holies;
Judea becomes part
of the Roman prov-
ince of Syria.

ca. 50 B.C. *Canonization of the*
Hebrew Old Testa-
ment; status of Song of
Songs, Esther, and
Ecclesiastes disputed
until the middle of the
second century C.E.
Admonitions section
	of Ethiopic Enoch
Beginning and end
	of Ethiopic Enoch
Testaments of the
	Twelve Patriarchs

200

CHRONOLOGICAL TABLE

Letter of Jeremiah (Hebrew)	
Susanna	37–4 B.C. Herod I the Great
War Scroll (final version)	rules as king with Roman approval.
Prayer of Manasseh	
Life of Adam and Eve	31 B.C.–
Damascus Document B	A.D. 14 Octavian (Augustus after 27 B.C.)
A.D. 1 Assumption of Moses	
Slavonic Enoch	A.D. 26–36 Pontius Pilate
Letter of Jeremiah (Greek)	
IV Maccabees	
after A.D. 70 IV Ezra	A.D. 70 Titus takes
Baruch (final version)	Jerusalem.
A.D. 76 Sibyllines iii. 46ff., 143-44	
Apocalypse of Baruch (Greek)	
ca. A.D. 90 Apocalypse of Baruch (Syriac)	
A.D. 100 Christian redaction of the Testaments	A.D. 135 Fall of Beth Ter; End of the Bar
ca. A.D. 600 Christian redaction of Slavonic Enoch.	Kochba revolt under Hadrian; Aelia Capitolina

201

Supplementary Bibliography

Because the literature on this subject is readily accessible through standard indexes and bibliographies, only some of the more important publications issued after the German edition of this work are cited here.

Alonso, Schökel L. *Proverbios y Eclesiastico*. Los libros sagrados. Antiguo Testamento, 8:1. Madrid, 1968.

————. *Rut, Tobias, Judit, Ester*. Los libros sagrados. Antiguo Testamento, 5. Madrid, 1973.

Bardtke, H. "Literaturbericht über Qumran," *ThR*, XXXVII (1972):97–120, 193–219; XXXVIII (1973): 257–91; XXXIX (1974):189–221.

Barthélemy, D. *Konkordanz zum hebräischen Sirach*. Göttingen, 1973.

Bartlett, J. R. *The First and Second Books of the Maccabees*. Cambridge Bible Commentary: New English Bible. Cambridge, 1973.

Beckwith, R. T. "Modern Attempts to Reconcile the Qumran Calendar with the True Solar Year," *RQ*, VII (1970):379–96.

Charlesworth, J. H. "Renaissance of Pseudepigrapha Studies," *Journal for the Study of Judaism*, II (1971):107–14.

Clarke, E. G. *The Wisdom of Solomon*. Cambridge Bible Commentary: New English Bible. Cambridge, 1973.

Dancy, J. C. *The Shorter Books of the Apocrypha*. Cambridge Bible Commentary: New English Bible. Cambridge, 1972.

JUDAISM OUTSIDE THE HEBREW CANON

Davenport, G. L. *The Eschatology of the Book of Jubilees.* Leiden, 1971.

Denis, A. M. *Introduction aux pseudépigraphes grecs d'Ancien Testament.* Leiden, 1970.

Driver, G. R. "Mythology of Qumran," *JQR,* LXI (1971):241–81.

Enslin, M. S. *The Book of Judith.* Jewish Apocryphal Literature, 7. Leiden, 1972.

Janssen, E. *Das Gottesvolk und seine Geschichte.* Neukirchen, 1971.

Jonge, H. J. de. "Die Text überlieferung der Testamente der zwölf Patriarchen," *ZNW,* LXIII (1972):27–44.

Jongeling, B. *A Classified Bibliography of the Finds in the Desert of Judah 1958–1969.* Leiden, 1971.

Kümmel, W. G. *Jüdische Schriften aus hellenistisch-römischer Zeit.* Gütersloh, 1973–.

Klign, A. F. J. "Sources and the Redaction of the Syriac Apocalypse of Baruch," *Journal for the Study of Judaism,* I (1970):65–76.

Lamadrid, A. G. *Los descubrimientos del Mar Muerto.* 2nd ed. Madrid, 1973.

Lamparter, H. *Die Apokryphen.* Stuttgart, 1972.

Lebram, J. C. H. "Die literarische Form des vierten Makkabäerbuches," *Vigiliae Christianae,* XXVIII (1974):81–96.

Middendorp, T. *Die Stellung Jesu Ben Siras zwischen Judentum und Hellenismus.* Leiden, 1973.

Milik, J. T. "Problèmes de la littérature Hénochique à la lumière des fragments araméens de Qumrân," *HThR,* LXIV (1971):333–78.

———. "Recherches sur la version grecque du livre des Jubilés," *RB,* LXXVIII (1971):545–57.

Moore, C. A. "On the Origins of the LXX Additions to the Book of Esther," *JBL,* XCII (1973):382–93.

———. "Toward the Dating of the Book of Baruch," *CBQ,* XXXVI (1974): 312–20.

Myers, J. M. *I and II Esdras.* Anchor Bible, 42. Garden City, 1974.

Philonenko, M. "La littérature intertestamentaire et le Nouveau Testament," *RSR*, XLVII (1973):270–79.

Sanders, J. A. "Dead Sea Scrolls: A Quarter Century of Study," *BA*, XXXVI (1973):110–48.

———. "Palestinian Manuscripts, 1947–1972," *JJSt*, XXIV (1973):74–83.

Snaith, J. G. *Ecclesiasticus*. Cambridge Bible Commentary: New English Bible. Cambridge, 1974.

Strugnell, J. "Notes en marge du volume V des Discoveries in the Judaean Desert of Jordan," *RQ*, VII (1970):163–276.

Surburg, R. F. *Introduction to the Intertestamental Period*. St. Louis, 1975.

Thomas, J. D. "The Greek Text of Tobit," *JBL*, XCI (1972):463–71.

Turdeanu, E. "Les Testaments des Douze Patriarches en slave," *Journal for the Study of Judaism*, I (1970):148–84.

Unnik, W. C. van, ed. *La littérature juive entre Tenach et Mischna*. Journées bibliques de Louvain, 20. Leiden, 1974.